Advance Praise for
Living Spiritually in a Material World

"Before shelves were warping under the weight of self-help books, before the caring industries were promising happiness via therapy or pills, many Americans sought guidance and wisdom from—of all people—Christian college presidents. Lewis Andrews unearths the story of how these religious, educational, and social leaders came to be spiritual instructors, and he shows how their advice can still help us lead lives of greater courage, resilience, and grace."

—*Adam Keiper, Books & Arts editor,* The Weekly Standard

"*Living Spiritually in the Material World* is a surprising and delightful book. Lewis Andrews has done us a great service by discovering and reflecting on classic insights that will help us, even today, to live with spiritual meaning in our everyday lives."

—*Dr. Mark Roberts, executive director, Max De Pree Center for Leadership, Fuller Theological Seminary*

"Few appreciate the connection between higher education and the higher authority of the divine, but now comes Lewis Andrews with this fascinating study of early college presidents in U.S. history and how their deep faith nurtured their work as our nation's top educators. They not only educated our Founders; they also provided useful guidance for spiritual wisdom which Andrews translates for today's modern audience."

—*Mike McCurry, professor/director, Wesley Theological Seminary and former State Department/White House spokesman (1993–98)*

"*Living Spiritually in the Material World* goes beyond self-help to real personal transformation."

—*Tony Ingle, president, General Dynamics*
Faith and Hope Employee Resource Group

"With wisdom and spiritual teachings from America's earliest college presidents, Lew Andrews has given us a thoughtful book of lessons to help make sense of today's turbulent and confusing times."

—*Dr. Laura Forese, chief operating officer,*
New York Presbyterian Hospital

"'Stand at the crossroads and look; ask for the ancient paths, ask where the good way is, and walk in it, and you will find rest for your souls' was written by the prophet Jeremiah but also accurately describes Dr. Lewis Andrews's new book *Living Spiritually in the Material World*. This uniquely important work describes spiritual wisdom from a different age in our country's history. Andrews presents the story of a group of men and women who truly understood how to live out their faith through their vocational calling, thereby shaping the ethical foundations of our nation for over three hundred years. A must read for those who want to find their way back to this important path. This is a very important part to the 'faith and work' story that has not been told."

—*Hugh Whelchel, executive director of the*
Institute for Faith, Work & Economics

"*Living Spiritually in the Material World* is very important; dealing with faith in the US specifically from a cultural and historical perspective. Well researched and thoughtful efforts to bring to light what we can all sense but didn't have the objective perspective."

—*Jeff Rogers, chairman, OneAccord Capital*

"A willed ignorance of the importance of faith weakens our democracy. In *Living Spiritually in the Material World*, Lewis Andrews sketches out what could make our communities stronger: faith, community, civility."

—*Amity Shlaes, former member of the* Wall Street Journal *editorial board and author of* Coolidge

"An engaging and enlightening book that combines the moral and spiritual wisdom of previous generations of college and university presidents in America with findings of contemporary psychology. The author combines spiritual and theological reflection with substantive analysis, as he seeks to address ten specific issues related to *Living Spiritually in the Material World*."

—*Dr. Corwin Smidt, senior fellow, Henry Institute for the Study of Christianity and Politics*

"At a time of national moral decline, when there is growing skepticism about the value of our militantly secular and hideously expensive institutions of higher education, Lewis Andrews's *Living Spiritually in the Material World* will turn your head with a dazzling and hopeful insight. Higher education in America used to be one of our country's principal sources of moral and spiritual wisdom, and perhaps most amazing of all, it was the presidents of American colleges and universities who provided most of that wisdom. I knew this in a general way before reading his book—but I was bowled over by the volume, the passion, and the eloquence with which our country's earliest collegiate leaders made the case for the moral education of their charges. Could higher education experience a moral renaissance, if something resembling that moral center at the top were to be restored? This book strongly suggests that the answer might be 'Yes.'"

—*Prof. Wilfred M. McClay, G.T. and Libby Blankenship Chair in the History of Liberty, University of Oklahoma*

"For nearly four centuries, U.S. colleges and universities were led by clergymen presidents. Dr. Lewis Andrews draws on his deep knowledge of these presidents' lectures and sermons to explore their roles as leading public intellectuals and teachers of moral philosophy. At a time when higher education is often seen as preparation for career, in *Living Spiritually in the Material World*, Dr. Andrews reminds us that colleges and universities should also prepare students to be of service to their community and engage in life's deepest questions."

—*Jacqueline Pfeffer Merrill, director, Campus Free Expression Project, Bipartisan Policy Center*

"*Living Spiritually in the Material World* is timely, fresh, honest, deep, and arresting. It brilliantly recovers, for our benefit today, the moral wisdom of Christian college presidents in centuries past, before American education lost its way by claiming to be value neutral. An unlikely page-turner, deftly blending history, biography, theology, psychology, storytelling, social commentary, and good counsel. A book to read, reread, mark up, ponder on, and live by."

—*John Andrews (no relation to author), former president, Colorado State Senate*

"There was a time when students heard their college president share some version of Augustine's prayer to God: 'you have made us for yourself, and our heart is restless until it rests in you.' Dr. Lewis M. Andrews bemoans the fact that such spiritual and psychological wisdom is rarely heard in the academy today, and shows how modern studies bear witness to the need for and the benefit of such a message."

—*Dr. David L. Weeks, dean of the Honors College at Azusa Pacific University*

LIVING SPIRITUALLY
IN THE
MATERIAL WORLD

*The Lost Wisdom for Finding Inner
Peace, Satisfaction, and Lasting
Enthusiasm in Earthly Pursuits*

LEWIS M. ANDREWS, PH.D.

FIDELIS
BOOKS

A FIDELIS BOOKS BOOK
An Imprint of Post Hill Press
ISBN: 978-1-64293-390-1
ISBN (eBook): 978-1-64293-391-8

Living Spiritually in the Material World:
The Lost Wisdom for Finding Inner Peace, Satisfaction, and Lasting
Enthusiasm in Earthly Pursuits
© 2020 by Lewis M. Andrews, Ph.D.
All Rights Reserved

All Scripture taken from the King James Version (KJV) and is public domain in the United States.

Post Hill Press
New York • Nashville
posthillpress.com

Published in the United States of America

For Kate and Zach

CONTENTS

*What we profoundly and constantly need is...
knowledge of the laws of the spiritual world,
and not some meteoric flash that may seem for a
moment to dispel the darkness, but leaves us, in the
end, more confused than ever.*

—John Bascom,
president of the University of Wisconsin
(1874–1887)[1]

*Real religion is the offering up of each man's life,
in its concrete setting, day by day, hour by hour,
moment by moment, to the guidance and keeping
of God. Thus each man's religion, like his life, is
individual, unique.*

—William DeWitt Hyde,
president of Bowdoin College
(1885–1917)[2]

These millions of man-made gods, these myriads of personal idols, must be broken up and destroyed, and the heart and mind of man brought back to a comprehension of the real meaning of faith and its place in life.

—Nicholas Murray Butler,
president of Columbia University
(1902–1945)[3]

As your character is, so will your destiny be.

—Mark Hopkins,
president of Williams College
(1836–1872)[4]

INTRODUCTION

It is this great and fundamental truth—that there is no true rest for the soul of man except in God—that needs to be proclaimed at all times and everywhere. Look at the restlessness of individuals and of society.... See the world busy in letting down empty cups into wells that are dry, or drinking to "thirst again;" see individuals passing through all the stages of poverty and of wealth, of neglect and of distinction...there is, and there will be "overturning, and overturning, and overturning," till men find the true rest of their souls, and He whose right it is shall assume His spiritual and perfect reign.

—Mark Hopkins, president of
Williams College (1836–1872)[5]

[How] many there are who, if challenged, will confess that [though] they have not given up the belief in...God, [they] yet live as though they

neither had nor sought a close relationship with Him. Receiving all bounties from Him, they yet live as though they had no relationship except with their fellowman. They may strive to be not only honorable in their dealings with others, but even to be generous and philanthropic. But so far as we can discover, their souls give no sign of running out with gratitude towards the Giver of all good gifts to them.

—James B. Angell, president of the University of Michigan (1871–1909)[6]

Angels minister to one whose masterful determination refuses the beguilement of secondary things.

—Melancthon Woolsey Stryker, president of Hamilton College (1892–1917)[7]

The Great Paradox

It is largely forgotten today, but for nearly three centuries, from the founding of Harvard College in 1636 right up until the early twentieth century, there was a highly educated and remarkably talented group of ministers whose lives were dedicated to teaching what it means to live spiritually in the whole of one's life—not just at home or in church, but at work, in community activities, through politics, and even during war or natural disasters. This was the era when virtually every American college or university was sponsored by a major Christian denomination and when their presidents were clergy, especially selected for the ability to clarify religious and spiritual ideas.

The times in which these early college presidents lived were not nearly as skeptical as our own, but it was certainly not for lack of testing. The first European settlers endured famines, deadly diseases, and, in the northern colonies, often brutal winters. Later came the War for Independence, pitting colonists against relatives from their mother country, then a bloody Civil War, and finally a world war so traumatic survivors came to be known as "the Lost Generation."

The early twentieth century—the end of the Christian college presidents' time in office—was challenging in still another way, as the Industrial Revolution produced a massive migration from America's farmlands to its cities. Families were uprooted, once-cherished customs abandoned, and many people found themselves in coarse urban surroundings with scant support for their childhood religious beliefs.

Throughout this entire three-century period, the nation's college presidents saw their mission as providing students with the insight needed to recognize and follow God's guidance in the larger world beyond home and school. As ministers, they were acutely aware of the great religious challenge vividly described at the very beginning of the Old Testament and later illustrated in the rise and fall of so many civilizations: to resist the illusion that the worldly technologies can be productively employed independently of God's service.

As far back as *Genesis* 1:28, Scripture promised that those faithful to the Lord would be blessed with ever-greater knowledge of how to harvest the world's bounty for their own comfort and enjoyment. "Be fruitful, and multiply," it said, "and replenish the earth, and subdue it: and have dominion over the fish of the sea, and over the fowl of the air, and over every living thing that moveth upon the earth." *Isaiah* 40:31 is just one of many subsequent passages which repeat this pledge, declaring that they who "wait upon the Lord shall renew *their* strength; they shall mount up with wings as eagles; they shall run, and not be weary; *and* they shall walk, and not faint."

But Scripture also warned that material knowledge misleads people into imagining they can get along just fine without Divine guidance, either by compartmentalizing their worship to weekly sermons and a few annual rituals or, even worse, by imagining they could become their own gods, deciding what is worth having and how best to acquire it. "Seek not after your own heart and your own eyes," *Numbers* 15:39 clearly cautions. And in 1 *Corinthians* 3:18–19: "Let no man deceive himself. If any man among you seemeth to be wise in this world, let him become a fool, that he may be wise. For the wisdom of this world is foolishness with God."

America's early academic leaders had many ways of describing humanity's perennial tendency to ignore its Benefactor. Some, like Milwaukee-Downer College co-founder Catharine E. Beecher (1850–1852), spoke of it as a psychological deficiency. There is a "fatal disorder" which distorts "the consciousness of individuals in every age," she cautioned her students.[8] Others, including University of Wisconsin president John Bascom (1874–1887), were more inclined to see human pride as the natural reaction to an intellectual limitation. "The love of God is so comprehensive, takes such wide circuits, [and] is so patient in laying the foundations of good," he once wrote, "that men [will] easily become impatient of [trying to find] it and angrily deny its existence."[9]

But if the presidents used different wording, they had no doubt of self-sufficiency's danger, both to the person attempting it and to the larger society. "Partial allegiance…is almost the last thing in futility and dreariness," declared University of Denver chancellor William Fraser McDowell (1890–1899). "You can go the whole length with Him and live, live royally, live exultingly and victoriously, but if you only partially enthrone Him, or if you crown Him with mental reservations, you will not get far."[10] Many of McDowell's contemporaries took to paraphrasing Emory College's Atticus Greene Haygood (1876–1884), who warned that Christians do no greater damage to their souls than when they build "a high and mighty wall…along the whole frontier of [their] everyday life, separating it from [their] religious life as the Chinese wall was intended to separate the 'flowery kingdom' of the Celestials from savage deserts and more savage tribes beyond."[11]

Although Christian college presidents represented a variety of denominations, they were united in their determination to ensure the New World, which held so much promise, would not suffer the same fate as ancient Shinar, whose residents dared to build their own stairway to Heavenly happiness (*Genesis* 11:1–9), or of later Jerusalem, whose citizens so neglected God they were enslaved by the Babylonian king Nebuchadnezzar (*Jeremiah* 29:4–14). They instructed their students in the art of living spiritually everywhere in the world, so America's growing power and prosperity would hopefully never yield to the kind of self-destructive materialism that had ruined so many other nations.

The President's Seminar

Up until the American Revolution, when colleges were few and sparsely attended, the presidents conveyed their ideas in the context of a curriculum roughly comparable to a modern one. Students were expected to spend their first years studying many of the same subjects taught today: a foreign or classical language, English literature, geography, math, and science. But to graduate, they were also required to take a special seminar typically taught by the school's president.

The formal name for this course was *Moral Philosophy*, a phrase long used by European scholars to describe the role of Christian ethics in everyday life. But in America, it referred to something far more ambitious: a way of knowing and serving God everywhere in the larger society, regardless whatever obstacles, temptations, heresies, or even physical dangers one might encounter. Amongst themselves, students referred to this class as simply "the president's seminar."

Over time, as campus populations grew to the point where it was impractical for one person to conduct the same course for every undergraduate, college presidents began to reorganize their ideas into a series of Sunday sermons, which students attended regularly right up until the middle of the twentieth century. These sermons became, in turn, chapters of self-help books designed to help any Christian wishing to live his or her faith to its fullest. On campus, they were used as texts for America's first psychology courses, typically taught by ministers with practical experience in social work. Off campus, the books were read as eagerly by shopkeepers and farmers as they were by the most accomplished professionals.

Many of the most popular authors—Mark Hopkins of Williams College (1836–1872), Princeton's James McCosh (1868–1888), and Yale's Noah Porter (1871–1886)—became nationally admired figures, in great demand as lecturers and guest speakers. DePauw College's first president, Matthew Simpson, was a trusted advisor to Lincoln;[12] and two 1885 debates on religious education between McCosh and Harvard president Charles Eliot were considered important enough to be covered on the front pages of newspapers across the country.[13] *Acres of Diamonds*, based on a sermon by Temple University president Russell Conwell (1887–1925), is still in print and remains one of the most influential books ever published.

Indeed, it is hard to overstate the presidents' influence. Their work inspired the success of hundreds of social service organizations, including the Young Men's Christian Association (YMCA), the American branch of the Salvation Army (which began in England), and the precursors of modern substance abuse programs such as Alcoholics Anonymous.[14] The presidents convinced many mental hospitals to end their historically callous warehousing of inmates and adopt a more humane approach, which came to be known as "moral treatment."[15]

Such was the respect afforded US college presidents that those who traveled abroad were often asked to extend their stays and talk to locals about what it meant to live as Christians. When it was learned, for example, that Amherst president Julius

Hawley Seelye would stop in Bombay on his 1872–73 around-the-world tour, educated Hindus prevailed upon him to deliver a series of lectures titled "The Way, the Truth, and the Life," which were published widely throughout India.[16]

In the late nineteenth century, as US colleges and universities liberalized their admissions policies, admitting students from competing denominations and even from other faiths, the off-campus interest in the presidents' religious guidance only grew. The relaxation of the doctrinal differences previously separating the various Protestant churches meant spiritual advice from, say, a Methodist college president could now be more comfortably received by a Presbyterian or Congregational audience. At a time when many European intellectuals were flirting with atheistic Marxism and materialistic interpretations of Darwin, thoughtful Americans were clearly enamored of a more spiritual outlook.

It was not a coincidence that in 1893, when Chicago hosted a large trade fair to celebrate the four hundredth anniversary of Columbus' discovery of the Americas, the biggest and most anticipated program was the World's Parliament of Religions—an unprecedented gathering of seven thousand believers representing faiths from every part of the world. For seventeen days, the proceedings continued to be front page news from coast to coast.

Admittedly, some Christians saw this seemingly indiscriminate welcoming of other religions as a bit too tolerant. The General Assembly of the Presbyterian Church passed a resolution late in 1892 disapproving of the coming convention—although many members attended anyway. Further opposition came from England's Archbishop of Canterbury and Roman Catholic clergy on the Continent.[17]

But for the early college presidents, the event was the perfect opportunity to highlight how much their own country's broadly Christian culture achieved in the short time since the nation's founding, to address the curiosity of admirers in places as far away as India and China, and to provide the growing number of American missionaries with a deeper understanding of the cultures they hoped to influence. It was in this spirit that several Gospel hymns and the "Hallelujah Chorus" from Handel's *Messiah* were scheduled to frame the final presentations.[18]

Indeed, by the turn of the twentieth century, the spiritual wisdom of America's clerical college presidents became so widely accepted it became the basis for a popular therapeutic movement, one nearly eclipsing the rise of what we now think of as modern psychiatry. It began in 1905 when a doctor at Massachusetts General Hospital asked Elwood Worcester, an Episcopal priest at Boston's Emmanuel Church, to instruct poor tuberculosis patients on the medical advantages of rest, nutrition, and fresh air. This initial collaboration between a prestigious medical school and an Episcopal clergyman, well-versed in the teachings of the Christian college presidents, eventually led to a church-based clinic to train lay therapists to help local parishioners deal more effectively with everyday emotional problems.

In 1908, Worcester, along with another Episcopal priest named Samuel McComb, and a neurologist from nearby Tufts University, published *Religion and Medicine, the Moral Control of Nervous Disorders*, which was so popular it ran through nine printings its first year. The establishment of spiritually-oriented mental health clinics, which came to be known as the Emmanuel Movement, quickly spread to nearby churches in Boston's fashionable Back Bay, then to parishes throughout Massachusetts, and finally to Christian sanctuaries across the United States and even in some European cities.[19]

It was only Worcester's farsighted belief that spiritual failings contributed to heart disease, ulcers, and many other physical ailments—as well as his egalitarian conviction that psychotherapy should be freely available to all who need it[20]—that, by the early 1920s, provoked a sharp reaction from the medical community. Even so, enough ministers were inspired by the Emmanuel Movement that Worcester's methods became the basis of today's pastoral counseling programs at most Christian seminaries.[21]

The Great Regression

For all their success—indeed, because of it—the early college presidents inevitably had to confront the question of whether any spiritual teaching could ultimately prevent a prosperous society from succumbing to the allure of self-sufficient materialism. After all, to the extent a people remained faithful to God, the subsequent reward of ever-increasing technological prowess would only make the temptation to become one's own god that much stronger.

Williams College president Mark Hopkins (1836–1872) became one of the first to raise the issue publicly. "The power of man over nature is now greater than at any former period," he wrote. "[I]nvention is laying the labor of man upon the untiring elements; steam is hurrying forward our merchandise, and turning the wheels of our machinery, and reaching its long arms into the bowels of the earth." But if "the principles of [humanity's] moral and spiritual nature do not receive a correspondent expansion...we shall but furnish another, and a signal illustration of the truth of that saying of the wise man, 'The prosperity of fools shall destroy them.'"[22]

The paradoxical challenge of America's remarkable material success was a theme that increasingly surfaced in the graduation speeches of nearly all the Christian college presidents throughout the Industrial Revolution. "We live in a time of invention," president Caroline Hazard (1899–1910) opened a Wellesley baccalaureate address. "All the comforts of life are so increased, and the accessories of living are so multiplied, that we are accused of forgetting to live. The aids to a fuller and larger life become the ends of life itself, and...the weightier matters of the law are disregarded. In many respects, this is a true indictment.... [The] advance of civilization puts new tools at our disposal [and we] are so involved in processes that we forget the result."[23]

Yet it was not until the first decades of the twentieth century that the cultural influence of the early college presidents began to noticeably decline. There was no collapse of religion in the institutional sense. Americans still attended church in large numbers, had religious weddings, and wanted the clergy to say reassuring words before burying loved ones. But the ideal of following Divine guidance in all one's affairs was clearly yielding to the kind of compartmentalized faith Scripture always warned against: the embrace of a self-centered materialism in the world beyond home and communal worship.

It was a time when the clever manipulation of other people started to replace character development as the perceived key to happiness. When the unending accumulation of consumer goods—even to the point of going deeply into debt—became widely accepted. And when the mass media's fantasies of personal fulfillment exercised an almost hypnotic effect on how ordinary people wanted to look and act. All this is not to suggest there were few cases of manipulative self-centeredness prior to the early twentieth century, or few expressions of genuine faith thereafter, but a rapidly growing materialism was clear to F. Scott Fitzgerald, John Dos Passos, Sinclair Lewis, and many other keen observers of the period.

Much of the change was undoubtedly due to the First World War. Between 1914 and 1918, more than sixteen million combatants from twenty-seven nations died for what appeared in the end to be a pointless stalemate, with another twenty million wounded. To those American soldiers fortunate enough to come home, as well as to the loved ones of those who did not make it back, trust in a benevolent God became much harder to muster, especially as the advent of the automobile, broadcasting, and electric appliances seemed to make the direct pursuit of material pleasure a more reliable bet.

Along with the aftereffects of war came the promotion of psychological theories which challenged the presidents' claim of a necessary connection between spiritual values and emotional health—and which purported to show how any person could engineer his or her own happiness without any need of Divine intervention. A Johns Hopkins University professor named John Watson, whose experiments with animals demonstrating even longstanding habits could be altered with the right mixture of rewards and punishments, was especially persuasive in arguing that systematic programming is more powerful than prayer. "Give me a dozen healthy infants, well-formed, and my own specified world to bring them up in," he famously bragged, "and I'll guarantee to take any one at random and train him to become any type of specialist I might select—doctor, lawyer, artist, merchant-chief and, yes, even beggar-man and thief, regardless of his talents, penchants, tendencies, abilities, vocations, and race of his ancestors."[24]

Parallel developments in the field of brain chemistry added weight to the idea that human happiness flowed from biological conditions, which could be directly and precisely engineered. Noting what appeared to be the rejuvenating effects of opium, cocaine, and other psychoactive drugs, many researchers enthusiastically predicted a not-too-distant future when life satisfaction would be a simple matter of knowing what pill or injection to take. Even the famous Sigmund Freud, whose own theories on the connection between childhood traumas and later adult functioning were at best murky, contributed to the impression that mental health depended far more on mastering the material world than the spiritual one.

"Peculiar Cross"

Sadly, the ability of Christian college presidents to counter this rising religious skepticism was severely undermined by their own rapidly diminishing numbers, for by the early twentieth century they became the ironic victims of their own success. Their schools' programs in agriculture, medicine, architecture, history, chemistry, languages, and law waxed so outstanding many prospective students no longer applied to a college or graduate department with much consideration for its denominational affiliation. The result was that school trustees felt increasingly compelled to stop appointing presidents from the ranks of ministers and turn instead to the most capable fundraisers, effectively depriving the clergy of their most effective public platform.

It also did not help that the Carnegie Foundation for the Advancement of Teaching, which at the time had been giving matching grants to fund faculty retirements, had a strict policy of excluding colleges and universities under denominational control. For years, the Presbyterians and other mainline Protestant groups pled their case, but to no avail. Carnegie apparently felt a stricter separation of religion and education would lead to faster intellectual advancement, even though it was the education boom produced by Christian college presidents that created the need to better fund faculty retirements.[25]

Yet at the very moment when Americans seemed poised to accommodate the kind of religious compartmentalization that so disastrously undermined past civilizations, the last of the clerical college presidents remained optimistic their country's flirtation with psychological materialism would not last long enough to be fatal. Decades before, the presidents' predecessors invented the science of psychology in the belief it would show how the long-term effects of serving God, while impossible to trace in any detail, nevertheless converge on a life of serenity, fulfillment, and delight. With the eventual development of sophisticated research techniques, they believed, researchers would finally be able to track subjects over long enough periods to prove the wisdom of acting spiritually in all one's affairs.

What had come to pass in the meantime, the presidents thought, was not a scientific alternative to religion, but a seeming science that was not scientific enough—one so narrowly focused on the simple and immediate as to completely miss life's most important relationships. A misguided effort to tell the macro-story with micro-stories. And while the failure to go along with extrapolating the large from the small might leave steadfast Christians to bear what Yale president Theodore Woolsey (1846–1871) and Harvard president James Walker (1853–1860) regarded as the "peculiar cross"[26] of being thought intellectually backward, all attempts to engineer a better life short of faith in God would ultimately prove futile.

As it turned out, experimental evidence for the presidents' prediction was not long in coming. As early as 1936, Harvard-trained psychologist Saul Rosenzweig conducted the first in a long line of studies that would show that none of the newer materialistic psychologies were very effective when it came to the acid test of any self-help regimen: curing emotional problems.[27] Subsequent research demonstrated not only that people had a better chance of solving their personal difficulties by confiding them to a close friend than to a highly trained therapist, but those with the best chance for a long, healthy, socially-satisfying life were religious believers who attended church regularly.[28]

But while the idea of scientifically engineering human welfare had little to offer the average person, it did have a great deal to offer those who claimed to know how to do it. For, whereas the spiritual psychology of America's clerical college presidents placed responsibility for one's happiness in the hands of the individual—his or her moral choices reverberating in ways both personally and socially beneficial—its secular alternative promised an even better result from the employment of highly educated professionals. The unfortunate result was many of the credentialed occupations which came of age in the early twentieth century—public administrators, social workers, economists, criminologists, educators, urban planners, physicians, and other professionals—had a powerful incentive to promote the advantages of a materialistic outlook, regardless of its accuracy or utility.

This self-serving advocacy of psychological materialism may not have created a picture of the world that was either insightful or very useful, but it clearly nurtured a culture that encouraged its members to compartmentalize, abandon, and even ridicule the spiritual life for decades longer than the last of the Christian college presidents ever expected. Even the most glaring symptoms of social decay—the breakdown of the family, depression becoming the most commonly diagnosed medical disorder[29], and rising rates of mental illness in general[30]—were seen, not as warning signs of a dangerous metaphysical turn, but as reasons to invest even more in materialistic approaches to happiness. Still today, many remain oblivious to the connection between widespread dependence on secular expertise and the following: a record 24.6 million Americans regularly using illegal intoxicants, 30.2 percent of men and 16.0 percent of women binge-drinking at least once a month,[31] complaints of severe loneliness increasing from 20 to 40 percent of the population since 1980,[32] and an estimated 2.5 million Americans being addicted to painkilling opioids.[33]

The Spiritual Turning Point?

Only in recent years has the public become disenchanted, if not with the twentieth century's secular wisdom, then at least with the so-called "elites" who claim the technical expertise to employ it on their behalf. We see this most noisily in the rise of extremism at both ends of the political spectrum, but a more straightforward indicator is the results of polling on just how much Americans have come to mistrust their social institutions. Despite an improving economy, a 2016 survey by Gallup found people's faith in credentialed authority had dropped to historic lows.[34] A year later, the annual Edelman Trust Barometer revealed what it alarmingly called a "global implosion of trust."[35]

Technologically, Americans know they are more advanced than ever. They can communicate across the planet almost instantaneously, reside anywhere in climate-controlled comfort, enjoy an ever-expanding menu of recreations, and live on average to nearly twice the age of our not-so-distant ancestors.

And yet, when it comes to the question of what makes for a worthwhile life, there appears to be a dawning realization that nothing our social authorities have to offer can substitute for a long-lost confidence. No matter how clever, how articulate, how well-credentialed, or how respected by their colleagues our educated elites appear to be, we are haunted by the sense that something fundamental is missing...or even betrayed. In promising to show us how to live each moment for ourselves, our best and brightest have ignored what Hamilton College president Samuel W. Fisher (1858–1866) called the far more important ability to "live each moment for eternity."[36]

Even among social scientists, there is a growing movement to reexamine past research findings with an eye toward determining whether an overly materialistic bias may have colored supposed discoveries. And while this hardly represents a religious renaissance, it is at least a concession that much of what we have been assured is "established science" cannot in fact be replicated. Half the results ever published in peer-reviewed medical and social science journals are probably wrong, says John Ioannidis, head of the Meta-Research Innovation Center at Stanford University, which studies the reliability of previously-accepted scientific conclusions.[37]

Interestingly, the social science which has made the most spiritual progress in recent years is the very one that led the attack on the presidents' teachings more than a century ago. As far back as 1975, American Psychological Association president Donald T. Campbell was beginning to warn colleagues their profession's materialistic focus was turning out to be a serious mistake. There are good "reasons for modesty and caution in undermining traditional belief systems," he said in his leadership address to that year's convention.[38] Today, the Association's Division 36—the Society for the Psychology of Religion and Spirituality—has more than a thousand members, its own journal (*The Psychology of Religion and Spirituality*), and an impressive catalog of studies on the long-term impact of religious faith. Belief in God has proven to be associated with resilience to stress, a reduced likelihood of contracting either heart disease or diabetes, superior problem-solving skills, and (as we shall see) many other desirable traits.[39]

One striking development has been the complete turn-around in the way psychiatrists, psychologists, and social workers diagnose emotional complaints. Up until 1993, nearly one quarter of all the types of cases described in the *Diagnostic and Statistical Manual of Mental Disorders* (DSM), the standard reference used by both mental health professionals and insurance companies, were framed as symptoms of "neurotic religious thinking."[40] Not only has this anti-theological bias almost completely disappeared from the DSM, but the onset of a "spiritual emergency," or crisis of faith, is now regarded as a serious and legitimate emotional disorder.[41]

Equally impressive is the extent to which medical researchers have retreated from the idea that a person's sense of well-being can be pharmaceutically manufactured. In a remarkably under-reported 2002 study on the effectiveness of the six most widely prescribed antidepressants between 1987 and 1999, researcher Irving Kirsch (now at Harvard) admitted to only slight differences in the responses of patients taking the drugs versus those on placebos.[42]

More recently, Stanford University psychiatry professor David Burns has conceded, except for those suffering from schizophrenia, pharmaceuticals have little or no significant therapeutic effect.[43] Burns goes on to suggest the widespread use of antidepressants, anti-anxiety medications, and drugs purporting to improve attention is largely a waste of patients' time and money.

Dr. Len Sperry, clinical professor of psychiatry at the Medical College of Wisconsin, has perhaps summarized the emerging spiritual psychology better than anyone else. Up until the end of the nineteenth century, he writes, psychology was always understood to be "the study of the soul." Then, in a misguided quest to appear more scientific, "psychology sought to free itself from its roots in 'value-based' philosophy and become 'value-free' like physics and the biological sciences. Psychology also adopted a perspective and a method [which] were decidedly materialistic.... God, afterlife, free choice, and other spiritual phenomena [were treated as] false projections of the mind." But today there is a "shift under way" that, once again, argues those who live by the spiritual principles of America's Christian college presidents are, in fact, happier and healthier than those who do not.[44]

How to Live in the *Real* Real World

Does the growing disillusionment with psychological materialism and the institutions it gave birth to mean we are finally witnessing the spiritual rebound America's early college presidents predicted? That Christians seem unusually restless is perhaps a sign of imminent change. Growing numbers seek to insulate themselves and their families from secular influences through parochial or homeschooling, limiting their exposure to popular media, creating religious alternatives to public assistance and health-care programs, and even self-sufficient farming. Writer Rod Dreher has referred to this movement as the "Benedict Option,"[45] referring to the example of Saint Benedict of Nursia, whose support for the growth of monasteries in the sixth century shielded Christianity from the decadent materialism of later Roman society.

Other Christians, according to recent studies, are increasingly abandoning their mainstream church affiliations, with the percentage of Protestants who identify as a Methodist, Lutheran, or another traditional denomination falling from 50 percent as recently as 2000, to just 30 percent in 2016.[46] And while this development might appear to be an anti-religious one, it tends to be associated with more devotional activity, not less. The self-identified "non-denominational" is more likely to pray daily, to say religion is important to his or her life, to attend services weekly, and to read Scripture frequently. The quest of some Christians to reaffirm their religious traditions, and of others to streamline the essence of their faith, may well prove to be two expressions of the same underlying trend: a reversal of America's century-long compartmentalization of the religious life.

Whether the larger society is indeed on the verge of the spiritual revival predicted by the presidents, no one can say for certain. We can only wait on events. The eternal good news is the joy of serving God in the whole of one's life has never depended on majority opinion, even in the most cynical times. As the presidents often said, quoting *Colossians* 3:23–24, "And whatsoever ye do, do *it* heartily, as to the Lord, and not unto men; Knowing that of the Lord ye shall receive the reward of the inheritance: for ye serve the Lord Christ."

If America's early college leaders could wish any kind of self-help book for our own time it would almost certainly be the kind they wrote: a collection of essays aimed, not at reforming the world, but at improving one's self. Combining Scripture, historical anecdote, the reliable scientific knowledge of the day, and personal experience, it would educate the reader in the time-tested means for expressing one's faith in the larger world beyond family and church, especially in the face of inevitable doubts, insecurities, and diversionary temptations. Or as the University of Wisconsin president John Bascom (1874–1887) once put it, for rising above "the gains of life to life itself."[47]

It would also be a book Christians find especially helpful at work, the place where today's adults spend most of their waking hours, but with radically diminished guidance from a century of compartmentalized religious faith. Beyond being a too-long neglected site for one's own spiritual growth, the workplace is, day in and day out, the area where believers have the best opportunity to show non-Christians the difference a life devoted to God can make.

In the following pages, I have endeavored to write the kind of guide a Christian college president might have written, had he or she magically survived to our time. Drawing on nearly two decades of research on the lives and works of America's Christian college presidents, on a career spent writing about the relationship between spiritual values and emotional health, and on the personal insight from both using and ignoring such wisdom, I have written a book for those who intuit the necessity of serving God as widely and as often as possible. It should prove especially helpful to Christians called to careers, activities, and social settings where twentieth century secularism and religious skepticism still hold sway.

Because some of the quotes I use are more than 200 years old, a few words about my editing seem appropriate. First, in representing the old-time college presidents I have kept to their original texts as much as possible, except where minor changes in outmoded forms of punctuation were necessary for clarity. I have also retained the use of the masculine words *man* and *men* to mean *person* and *humanity*, since this practice was adopted in the nineteenth century as often by women college presidents as it was by their male counterparts.

Although it is likely obvious by now, I should probably confirm the dates bracketed after the name of a college president refer to time in office, not to his or her lifespan. I have also included a small number of quotes by old-time academics who never held the formal title of college president but who, as founders, chancellors, provosts or deans of large departments, assumed the duties of presiding officer in the early lives of their respective institutions.

Finally, it should be remembered that many of today's schools have gone through major name changes over the years. Princeton, for example, was once the College of New Jersey, just as DePauw University was previously Indiana Asbury University. Where an old school name is dramatically different from its most recent name, I use the later name to avoid confusion.

It is my humble hope that what follows will enable readers to more directly and effectively express God's will in their daily lives. And, in doing so, to experience more quickly and intensely the spiritual joy that can never be described by words alone. It is the joy that comes with realizing one's knowledge of the material world is but a convenient tool, not an objective fact—it is the ability to be active in the world without ever being limited by any merely human idea of it.

Reflection:

*But seek ye first the kingdom of God,
and his righteousness; and all these things
shall be added unto you.*
—Matthew 6:33

HOLD THE GREATEST THOUGHT

We need not say "God be with you," for God is with you. For you are with God. Only your own will can put God away from you and yourself away from God.... God is here; God is present. May this feeling and this faith give largeness to all your future. May this conviction make purpose higher and enthusiasm finer. May this assurance make you fearless without making you bold. May this belief make all your hopes and relations holy and Divine. May this truth aid you in finding and holding the talisman which shall keep your life simple and plain; and may this thought bless you by giving to your life holiness, completeness, and a sense of the infinite.

—Charles F. Thwing, president of Case Western Reserve University (1890–1921)[48]

Help me to hear Thy high and holy call in every homely duty and every humble task: in the drudgery of housekeeping; in the dreariness of accounts; in the difficulty of study; in the hardness of toil; in the competition of trade; in the claims of society; in the fight with appetite; in the struggle with poverty; in the management of wealth; in the love of friends; in courtesy to foes. In all the common experiences of life, help me to see Thy love going before me to point out the way my love must take.

—*William DeWitt Hyde,
president of Bowdoin College (1885–1917)*[49]

Do Thou enter, O Lord, for in Thy presence is fullness of joy. So may we find true communion with Thee; so may we find pardon and newness of life; so may we become fit instruments of Thy praise.

—*Caroline Hazard, president
of Wellesley College (1899–1910)*[50]

An Awakened Soul

Stephen Olin always loved his native Vermont. Born 1797 in the town of Leicester, where he attended the local district school, he later went on to Middlebury College and, while there, planned to land a local law internship after graduation.

But a serious illness in his senior year changed Olin's plans, and he was forced to find work in a warmer part of the country, where he hopefully could recover faster. Bidding farewell to his native hills, he headed for South Carolina, where he eventually found employment as principal of the Tabernacle Academy, a small Methodist private school in the Abbeville District.

As a young man, Olin never had very strong religious convictions. If anything, he was inclined to doubt God even existed. Yet now he found himself in this very devout community where he was expected not only to respect Christian beliefs, but to teach them to the local children. Among his many duties, Olin was required to open and close each school day with an inspirational prayer.

Clever as he was, Olin just assumed he could wing his way through any ceremonial obligations, feigning the appropriate solemnity. But as time passed, he became increasingly agitated. The problem, he knew, was conscience. So many decent people in the district were trusting him to be a good example for their children.

To Olin's surprise there was also the question of his own relationship with God who, after months of leading prayers and meditations, no longer seemed such an improbable being. Events in his life he once might have dismissed as coincidental now struck him as perhaps purposefully timed, and the daily task of selecting the Bible passages to be read at school was turning out to be far more intellectually stimulating than he initially expected.

Compelled to reconsider his religious skepticism, Olin undertook a systematic study of his nominal faith. And the more he read, the more his previous criticisms of Christianity began to seem either trivial or simply a holdover from his immature college days. Increasingly, the one-time atheist found himself convinced of a hidden power in the universe—so much so that he underwent what he called "a religious conversion" and, soon after, felt a call to prepare for the ministry.

Eventually becoming one of the most influential Methodist preachers of his day, Olin was appointed president of Randolph-Macon College in 1834 and, five years later, of Connecticut's Wesleyan University. In a sense, he did realize his dream of returning to New England, although not as the same religious skeptic who had graduated from Middlebury.

No More Important Habit

For those who strive to serve God in the course of a busy life, there is no more important habit than daily conjuring the thought of His presence. The very incongruity of such a notion, when contrasted with the outward show of worldly affairs, is a powerful reminder that our socially-conditioned beliefs about what the world is and how it operates are but crude simulations of a very different underlying reality. Regularly entertaining the thought which tells us our knowledge of the material world, while useful, is nowhere near complete—or even very accurate—opens the mind to the subtle spiritual influences it might otherwise ignore.

Even for a doubter like young Stephen Olin, the thought of a present God, which his job at the Methodist private school required him to resurrect almost daily, acted like a spiritual wedge, keeping his conscious mind available to hidden possibilities. As he later reflected, it was almost like a walking prayer which provided him access to a deeper wisdom.

Another early college president, Dartmouth College's Asa Dodge Smith (1863–1866), liked to illustrate the point by telling his students the story[51] of a religious naval officer whose ship came within sight of Ascension Island while cruising the South Atlantic. The volcanic wasteland of dried lava flows and cinder cones appeared as but a tiny speck on the horizon, yet this seasoned sailor was possessed by a strange desire to move toward it.

Knowing how odd such an order would appear to his crew, the captain at first struggled against the impulse, but the desire to approach the island only grew stronger. Finally, as his ship was starting to leave it behind, he gave in and told his lieutenant to put about.

The "order was obeyed, and the prow was turned towards the uninteresting little island," as Smith described the event, "and soon something of an unusual sort was perceived upon the shore." It was a white banner.

Recognizing the makeshift flag as the universal signal for distress, the crewmen quickly redoubled their efforts; and as the ship neared the island's rocky shore, a touching spectacle met their view. With little hope of rescue, sixteen starving men, already shipwrecked for many days, had set up a camp on the beach.

"How very possible is it," Smith would end the account by asking his students, "that down in the arcana of the [officer's] soul there was some special pressure of the Divine finger, reaching we know not what cell of memory, stirring we say not what wing of fancy, thrilling we aver not what chords of association, opening we affirm not what founts of feeling, yet giving such ultimate direction to the will, as wrought salvation for the perishing ones…?"

President Smith's point in telling of this unusual rescue was not to suggest every believer's intuition always produces a miraculous result…or even a result recognizable as beneficial. He was simply showing his students how the conscious acceptance of God's presence makes a person more available to the kind of guidance that might otherwise be dismissed while, at the same time, fortifying the courage needed to act on it.

Coming down to modern times, medical researchers such as Thomas Jefferson University Hospital's Dr. Andrew Newberg have shown just how profoundly the thought of a present God affects one's overall well-being. His own studies at the hospital's Marcus Institute of Integrative Health—Myrna Brind Center have shown people who live as if God were a constant companion are, on average, happier and healthier than those who do not. They are not only less likely to suffer from heart disease, high blood pressure, emphysema, cirrhosis, and other physical ailments, but are also less prone to psychological problems, such as anxiety, low self-esteem, loneliness, substance abuse, or thoughts of suicide.

Contrary to today's fashionable stereotype of the religious person as being narrow-minded or boringly traditional, Newberg finds the very opposite. Those who believe their God to be close at hand are more adventurous than most, willing to take greater personal and professional risks, and exhibit what psychologists term an "openness to personal growth."[52]

I can certainly think of many times in my own life when faith in a present God fortified my courage to risk the unconventional, but one incident from years back stands out. I was invited to appear for a half-hour interview on CNN's *Newsnight* program to discuss my recently published book, *To Thine Own Self Be True: The Relationship Between Spiritual Values and Emotional Health*, and arrived at the studio in Atlanta—only to discover my invitation was based on a misunderstanding. There had been a lot in the news around that time about some allegedly corrupt politician and, because my book dealt with ethics, the CNN producers thought my appearance would somehow tie into the general theme of "integrity in Washington."

At this point I could have made some vague, high-minded observation about a brewing scandal I really had not followed closely. Or I could have radically changed the subject to talk about what really interested me—the connection between spiritual values and emotional health—even though that was not what CNN's interviewer was expecting.

I still have a vivid memory of gritting my teeth, taking the plunge, and starting to talk on international television about the neglected importance of God in the modern world and the relationship between a person's character and his or her psychological well-being. Immediately, the interviewer began to stutter uncharacteristically, while his co-anchor went white and their colleagues behind the cameras froze in place, not knowing what to make of me.

I fully expected to be yanked off the air with some old-fashioned vaudevillian's hook. Yet when the commercial break came, the phone banks were flooded with interested viewers wanting more information, and the host relaxed into our conversation. Perhaps most tellingly, one of the behind-the-scenes cameramen who was covering me during the show shook my hand, thanked me for coming, and asked for a copy of my book.

Real Religion

One of the most familiar lines from Scripture has always been "Commit thy works unto the Lord, and thy thoughts shall be established." (*Proverbs* 16:3) Throughout history, Christians seeking success in some new business or difficult enterprise would ask God to bless their plans in hopes He might tilt future events to make their desired outcome more likely.

But as America's early college presidents would remind their audiences, the passage had a far more profound meaning, which is best understood in the context of another Biblical passage: "For my thoughts *are* not your thoughts, neither *are* your ways my ways, saith the Lord. For as the heavens are higher than the earth, so are my ways higher than your ways, and my thoughts than your thoughts." (*Isaiah* 55:8–9)

In other words, by committing one's efforts to a present God, the enlightened person seeks not the mere fulfillment of his or her narrow vision, but the incarnation of what God ultimately intends. This superior construction may superficially resemble the humanly designed plan, but will always call for inconvenient diversions, radical amendments, spontaneous actions, social offenses, and courageous decisions only the greatest thought can make possible.

It is for this reason, as Bowdoin College president William DeWitt Hyde (1885–1917) once remarked, practicing real religion and being a genuine non-conformist are one and the same thing. For by consistently offering up one's life "in its concrete setting, day by day, hour by hour, moment by moment, to the guidance and keeping of God," the person is liberated, not only from conventional ways of thinking, but also from conventional ideas of what it means to be unconventional. "Thus each man's religion, like his life, is individual, unique."[53]

Or to state it from a more cautionary perspective: If God is not first in our hearts, then someone or something else will be. There is a mental act of will that must be made every day—indeed, with extra effort on the most difficult days—to ensure human ideas of happiness do not have more power over us than the source of true and lasting happiness.

Conjuring God

As to exactly how one goes about keeping the thought of a present God in the background of a busy day, Scripture suggests considerable leeway for personal preference. There are many passages, for example, where God is approvingly referred to with symbols of human authority—a king, a father or mother, a prince, a lord, and even a commander of troops.

The *Bible* appears to be comfortable with any of these, just so long as they are understood to be metaphors for something beyond the human capacity to visualize. "Who only hath immortality, dwelling in the light which no man can approach unto; whom no man hath seen, nor can see…." (1 *Timothy* 6:16)

At the same time, there are Scriptural passages where God is described with more abstract and even tactile imagery. In ancient Hebrew and ancient Greek texts, for example, the words which we now translate as *Divine influence* also mean *wind* and *breath*.

Paul speaks of God as an all-pervading spirit. "For in him we live, and move, and have our being...." (*Acts* 17:28) We encounter something similar in *Psalm* 139, where the writer effectively asks, "Is there any place one could possibly go where God is not?" He then visualizes himself flying to the far corners of the universe, ascending to the heavens, then down toward the underworld, and finally branching out to the ends of the Earth. But everywhere he travels, the Divinity is also there.

Of course, the thought of Christ is always a suitable stand-in for God. And here, too, as the remarkable variety in the artistic depictions of Jesus down through the centuries would suggest, we have considerable leeway when attending to the Father through the Son.

As far back as God's response to Cain and Abel's offering in *Genesis* 4:1–8, it seems clear His approval of how we acknowledge His presence is determined less by strict adherence to any specific representation than by the appropriate attitude. He asks, more than anything else, that we strive to be sincere, grateful, respectful, and submissive.

If we remain unsure as to how to best depict the present God, it is helpful to note what representation produces the greatest upsurge in our energy or enthusiasm. The optimal reminder "that God is, and that He is in His world in His own day," Case Western Reserve president Charles F. Thwing (1890–1921) counseled students, is the one that gives "spring and buoyancy" to everyday activity.[54] The correct thought for each person, he said, is the one that most "awakens" the soul to His nearness.[55]

The Fatal Compromise

Perhaps the greatest misunderstanding about conjuring the thought of God's presence is this should only be done by someone whose faith is constant and untroubled by religious doubts. As we saw in Stephen Olin's case, it is often the person with a wavering faith who is likely to experience the most immediate benefit from holding the greatest thought.

Incoming freshmen to early America's colleges and universities were often surprised to discover their adolescent inclination to challenge religious orthodoxy, especially where it restricted access to alcohol, sex, and gambling, was not only tolerated by their teachers, but often encouraged. Williams' Mark Hopkins (1836–1872), Princeton's James McCosh (1868–1888), Yale's Noah Porter (1871–1886), and Amherst's Julius Hawley Seelye (1876–1890) were especially noted for promoting religious controversy in their classes.

As ordained ministers, these presidents knew the active questioning of religious belief was an ironically effective, if unintended, way to keep God present. They were taught the very word *religion* was derived from an ancient verb meaning "to ponder"—and the seemingly noncommittal decision of a skeptic like Olin to simply study Christianity, however critically, could open the way to constructive life changes.

"There is less to fear," retired Harvard president James Walker (1853–1860) wrote in 1879, "from an avowed and active skepticism than from a skepticism which is unacknowledged and merely passive…. An active skepticism will often cure itself, work itself clear of its difficulties…. [It] does not imply indifference to the truth, nor prevent men from discriminating; so that while it leads them to deny this thing or doubt that, it leaves their confidence in other things unimpaired and perhaps strengthened and quickened…."[56]

One of the most persuasive demonstrations of this principle in our own time involved the late psychologist Albert Ellis, who early in his career became a well-known critic of organized religion, claiming it caused congregants to suffer needless guilt, depression, anxiety, and many other emotional problems. Yet for all his heretical pronouncements, Ellis remained frequently, if antagonistically, engaged with God, sometimes by debating well-known Christian psychotherapists, such as Allen Bergin, and at other times by writing pamphlets with titles like *The Case Against Religiosity*.

Although he never revealed exactly how or when it finally happened, the result of his unrelenting attacks on both Judaism and Christianity was a turnaround so complete he eventually took to describing the *Bible* as "a self-help book that has probably enabled more people to make more extensive and intensive personality and behavioral changes than all professional therapies combined." Ellis even went on to co-author a book on counseling patients with relevant excerpts from Scripture.[57]

Far more harmful than honestly questioning God's existence is accepting His reality, but as some remote being who long ago set the universe in motion, who occasionally intervenes to lay down some basic laws or perhaps perform a few convincing miracles, but who otherwise leaves us pretty much on our own. Such an outlook may allow the nominal believer to enjoy the occasional Sunday service and feel vaguely comforted at important life passages, such as weddings and funerals, but deadens the mind's sensitivity to spiritual inspiration.

Ultimately, as Yale president Noah Porter (1871–1886) warned almost a century and a half ago, the absence of a present God leaves even self-described believers with the impression of living in a world no grander than it appears, in a place where one's fate is determined almost exclusively by the ability to manipulate people and things. When that happens, Porter would warn graduating seniors, it is only a matter of time before life "seems hardly worth living for what life itself can give. At best, it becomes a dull farce or a weary tragedy; and, whether it is either, the play had better be over [for life has become] a bewildered dream, from which there is no waking; and the sooner we sink into a dreamless sleep, the better."[58]

An unusually inventive mind or the willingness to indulge extreme sensuality might keep such grim sentiments in check for a while, Porter conceded. But without the regular reminder that so-called reality is but a navigational convenience, boredom and disillusionment inevitably triumph. Or as a later president, DePauw University's Francis John McConnell (1909–1912) liked to put it, "intellectual speculation and emotional thrill" are weak substitutes for a present God.[59] Eventually the sense of missing something fundamental—of failing's one's purpose without knowing why—becomes the source of increasing dissatisfaction.

It is certainly no coincidence the period following the declining influence of the Christian college presidents in the early twentieth century, while far more technologically advanced than the era preceding, has nevertheless been characterized by high rates of mental illness, alcoholism, drug addiction, and family breakup, as well as by a narcissistic culture of insatiable self-absorption. Material invention may provide a wealth of distractions and physical comforts, but it is no substitute for the comfort of Divine companionship.

There is a particularly unfortunate tendency in our own time for many Christians to allow a popular scientific theory called the "Big Bang" to limit their concept of God's presence. Because our current representation of the material universe suggests it took shape around 13.8 billion years ago, exploding from a tiny point to its present size, millions of believers have tacitly accepted the idea God got things going in a single burst of energy but wanted little continuing role in whatever came after.

A far more helpful—and scientifically accurate—use of astronomy is to remind ourselves that any generally accepted description of existence is nothing more than the best tool yet discovered for managing humanity's way in the dark without stumbling too badly. In ancient times, it worked well to see oneself living on a flat Earth at the very center of creation; today it works even better to imagine ourselves on a modest, spherical-shaped planet circling an obscure star. Who knows what reality will most practically suit our descendants?

Indeed, the more deeply we try to understand the nature of our physical reality, the more unlikely and improbable it appears. Rocks, trees, and other forms of "solid" matter turn out to be buzzing collections of tiny energy waves, separated by relatively vast expanses of emptiness. Outer space is bent, time varies with speed, and a quantum particle can influence a distant neighbor without having any measurable connection to it.

While there is nothing in modern science to conclusively prove the existence of a present God, it is equally true modern science gives us no reason to doubt it. If what we call reality is simply the most reliable tool yet found for representing what we do not know for certain, then it is not the accuracy of the tool which determines our well-being, but how we relate to it: as ultimate truth or the context in which we serve something greater than ourselves.

God's Companions

The early college presidents who traveled frequently to give public lectures and guest sermons around the country were always impressed by how easy it was to identify those men and women who sustained the thought of a present God. They were the ones who displayed exceptional enthusiasm for whatever task was at hand, the people who had a quiet—almost otherworldly—self-confidence, the people who showed remarkable resilience, no matter what their limitations or challenges.

Such people, the presidents knew, lived in many countries and during every historical period, although early America seemed to have attracted and bred a disproportionately high percentage of them. They were not confined to any income group, class, occupation, or educational pedigree. Nor were they identified by the supposed importance of their work. Some might appear stylish, while others cared little for contemporary fashion.

What they did have in common was the habit of valuing an activity, not according to its profitability, its social status, or by any other external measure, but by its spiritual frame. Like the prophet Enoch in *Genesis* 5:22, they *practiced the presence of God.*

At some point in their lives, these people learned that making good choices is less a matter of exhaustively analyzing the various alternatives than it is about maintaining a consciousness of God's presence. Experience taught them the difference between the person who achieves something of real value and the one who does not is the former's consciously enforced availability to Divine influence.

They came to see the design of the Lord's Prayer was no accident. It begins, not with "give us this day our daily bread," "forgive us our debts," or "lead us not into temptation" but with, "hallowed be Thy name. Thy kingdom come, Thy will be done in earth, as it is in heaven." (*Matthew* 6:9–13)

Life teaches anyone with the courage to test it that the more one holds the greatest thought, the more short-term successes or failures seem but small things when compared to what is achieved overall. "[K]nock, and it shall be opened unto you." (*Matthew* 7:7)

By acknowledging the obvious—if God is, He must be everywhere—we gain the confidence of knowing, even in hardship and suffering, no soul is abandoned who acknowledges His company. In the words of the University of Chicago's first president, William Rainey Harper (1891–1906), "Religious life is largely the outward expression of thought, and thought is most ideal when it is thought of God."[60]

Reflection:

...be ye transformed by the renewing of your mind,
that ye may prove what is that good, and
acceptable, and perfect, will of God.
—Romans *12:2*

LESSON TWO:

TRUST YOUR INTUITION

Do you feel or hear or perceive some great, still voice in your inmost soul saying, go to this or that work? Obey that voice at the risk of your life. When you have hushed it for [a time], does it come drumming in your ears again in the still hour of contemplation or the quiet hours of the night season? You must obey that voice, or you are a ruined man.

—*Braxton Craven, president of Duke University (1842–1863 and 1866–1882)*[61]

It is quite obvious that most men practically underrate the influence of the heart *compared to that of the* head *on success and happiness. It is also easy to account for the mistake and at the same time to show that it is a mistake....*

—*James Walker, president of Harvard College (1853–1860)*[62]

When we turn our thoughts inward upon ourselves, not in the way of logical reflection, but in the way of intuitional perception, then it is preeminently that [God's] voice is heard.... There is in every man a consciousness of God, which is as original and as fundamental as is the consciousness of self; and this is the most direct and the most cogent argument for the existence of God that may anywhere be found. If that fails, or is ignored, then indeed is the light in the [person] turned to darkness....

—*John Williamson Nevin, president of Franklin and Marshall College (1866–1876)*[63]

GPS for the Soul

Braxton Craven, who served as the second president of the institution that became Duke University from 1842 to 1863 and then again from 1866 to 1882, was likely one of the busiest men in North Carolina. When not engaged in administrative work or teaching subjects as diverse as ancient mythology, chemistry, geology, and economics, he was making astronomical calculations for *Turner's Almanac*, writing legal contracts for neighbors, refereeing legal disputes throughout Randolph County, running his sizeable farm, and often taking personal charge of repairs to the school. He even found time to write two novels under the pen name of Charlie Vernon, one an historical drama, the other a crime thriller based on a real-life murder of the time.

Yet Dr. Craven had one striking peculiarity. Often, he would encounter people he knew on the street and not stop to speak with them or even lift his eyes from the ground. Fellow professors could pass him in the hallways without his seeming to be aware of them. New students eager to follow up on something he said in class quickly learned they needed to make an office appointment.

Craven was not antisocial. On the contrary, he had many close friends, including local politicians, judges, Duke alumni, and the very professors he so often appeared to ignore. One of his favorite sayings was the "cultivation of the genial, social, confiding, sympathetic, and philanthropic is one of the most important Christian duties."[64]

But like all the other early college presidents, Craven believed human consciousness played a unique function in the material world, serving as the bridge between God's will and everyday reality. "[The human body] is the only temple on earth that God inhabits," Craven would often remind his students. "He may write His name upon all created things…but He inhabits nothing on earth, but the human temple."[65] It was therefore incumbent on every Christian to listen attentively.

While not every early college president felt the need to be quite as protective of their introspective moods as Braxton Craven, they clearly viewed intuition as the most reliable source of Divine wisdom. Education and intelligence were, of course, highly prized; but God alone could see all ends from their beginnings and the subtle interconnectedness of seemingly disparate events. Only by being attentive to His will, then, could one hope to realize his or her greatest potential.[66] As it said in *Proverbs*

4:23, "Keep thy heart with all diligence; for out of it *are* the issues of life."

God's voice and *Divine light* were the two most common synonyms for intuition during the era of the early college presidents, but there were others. DePauw University president Matthew Simpson (1839–1848), a close confidant of Abraham Lincoln, called it the "ray from heaven" always shining upon the path God wishes us to follow.[67]

Working as he did with so many scientists and engineers, MIT president Henry Smith Pritchett (1900–1907) frequently compared intuitive wisdom to an energy field, hovering just beyond the range of measurable phenomena. "[We] know that there are [light wave] vibrations which lie below the red and above the violet which, falling upon the eye, give no vision, and are yet full of energy," he would tell his students. "Some such analogy holds in our minds. Our conscious everyday relations lie within a limited range.... Below the threshold of our ordinary consciousness, as we well know, lies a consciousness of another sort—sleep, for example." Above "ordinary everyday consciousness," he would continue, "lies a superlintral region of the human soul, like the ultra-violet part of the color spectrum...."[68]

When a Biological Computer Stands in for God

So strongly does most every person sense the wisdom of intuition that even the rise of psychological materialism during the first part of the twentieth century could not completely shake people's faith in it. Certainly, no storyteller of that time, or any since, would ever think to compose a tale in which the leading character triumphs by going against his or her gut instinct. It is only by having the courage to follow that "crazy hunch"—bravely defying the naysayers—will audiences accept the hero capturing the real murderer…finding true love…exposing the dark political conspiracy…thwarting the alien invasion…or making some important discovery.

We all have some sense of our intuitive powers, novelist Saul Bellow argued in his acceptance speech for the 1976 Nobel Prize in Literature. They are "powers we seem to derive from the universe itself." Most are "reluctant to talk about this," he added, "because there is nothing we can prove, because our language is inadequate," and because modern society has made people too embarrassed "to risk talking about it." But while "almost everyone keeps quiet about it…almost everyone is aware of it."

Knowing they could not convincingly refute the wisdom of intuition, the materialistic thinkers who succeeded the Christian college presidents tried the next best thing: they contrived a seemingly scientific explanation for intuition that did not take God into account. There were many variations on this approach, but they all went something like this: *There is a part of every brain which records the body's experiences, organizes them into a picture of the world, and makes its own assumptions about what is a smart or dumb move to make. All this goes on unconsciously except those times when this brain part calculates that the body has missed an important opportunity or gone off on an unwise tangent—at which point it interrupts the waking mind with an alert we call* intuition.

This attempt to explain spiritual guidance as an aspect of the brain's computer-like functioning is undoubtedly one of materialism's most clever ideas, persisting as it has until our own time.

Words like *process*, *compute*, and *simulate* have long become synonyms for *thinking*, while the more recent development of virtual reality and voice recognition technologies gives added credence to the idea that even the most sophisticated mental states can be explained materialistically.

All this sounds plausible enough until we realize treating intuition as the mere byproduct of organic computation is really a way to limit the authority of that computation. In other words, defining intuitive guidance in non-spiritual terms allows the worldview associated with those terms to become a check on that guidance.

Would David have taken on Goliath if he thought the impulse to do so was a flicker of his cerebral cortex and not the urging of an all-powerful God? Would George Washington have continued to lead his rag-tag forces against the greatest military power of his day unless he believed himself called by Providence? Would Florence Nightingale have so courageously invented the nursing profession during the bloody Crimean War without thinking herself on a Divine mission?

Outsized examples to be sure, but they make the point: a materialistic understanding of intuition limits our responses to precisely what God has intended we should be able to go beyond—what is safe, logical, sensible, and acceptable. The effect is to consign some of His most important calls—the ones in which He asks us to radically change course or to go beyond what currently seems possible—to the realm of fantasy, wish, immature desire, or even insanity. As none other than Albert Einstein is reported to have said, "The intuitive mind is a sacred gift and the rational mind is a faithful servant. We have created a society that honors the servant and has forgotten the gift."

Treating the mind as a biological computer is undoubtedly helpful to a brain surgeon; but turning that professionally useful metaphor into the ultimate description of the innerworkings of one's own mind effectively bleeds the courage to act when success is uncertain, undermines self-confidence with fears of what others might think, and makes every creative inspiration seem just a little riskier.

Some years back, a psychotherapist I was interviewing for a book on the connection between spiritual values and emotional health shared the story of a patient—a young woman who, for years, had attempted to cope with negative feelings about her father. At one point, finding herself torn between the familiar sense she should stay away from him and the unexpected intuition it would be helpful to learn more about his background, she made the choice to visit her father and tape a series of family history interviews. She did not ask him to justify any past actions or make up for the history of his emotionally hurtful comments, but simply to reveal more about his own childhood.

The result of the daughter's efforts, which included transcribing all the interviews, was a merging of their different perspectives on the events of her childhood and, with that, an unexpected reconciliation. In the end, her willingness to honor a "crazy impulse" prompted the father to confront certain realities he never previously faced, with the result that he was able to lower his defenses and apologize for how he mistreated her. The changes in both daughter and father could only have happened because she believed she had a higher spiritual calling to do what friends had judged unwise and had tried to dissuade her from doing.

There is an illustration of intuitive guidance in my own life which long ago convinced me how much more can be accomplished when we have a spiritual understanding of inspiration. It was more than twenty years ago and I was sitting on a plane, returning from a business trip. Paging through a magazine to pass the time, I came across an article about a Manhattan philanthropist who had donated a large sum of money to provide Catholic, Hebrew, Lutheran, and other parochial school scholarships, so poor and minority children in Albany, New York, could escape failing city schools.

"My home state of Connecticut could use something like that!" the thought struck me with unusual force. "Especially distressed cities like Hartford, Bridgeport, and New Haven."

At that time, I had neither the experience to run anything like a foundation to help inner-city kids, nor a fortune with which to fund it. But as I continued to talk about the idea with friends and at social gatherings, people came forward to volunteer their help in forming a board. We found an attorney willing to handle the paperwork and applied to the federal government for a charitable tax exemption.

Almost immediately, a series of remarkably improbable things began to happen, developments which left everyone involved with the impression some invisible power was clearing our way. For example, the attorney who filed for our tax-exempt status with the IRS had a partner in the trust and estates division of his law firm, who, it turned out, had a wealthy client wanting to fund school reform in Hartford. Within days of receiving IRS

approval for our fledgling charity—a charity with no employees and a volunteer board—we received a check for $1 million
from this client as well as offers from radio and television sta-
tions across Connecticut to promote our scholarships. We also
received an endorsement from the mayor of Hartford and editorial support from many of the state's newspapers. A year later,
the same wealthy donor gave us another check—this time for
$2 million—and today, the Children's Educational Opportunity
Foundation of Connecticut annually provides more than 400
matching scholarships to needy students in four of my home
state's most distressed cities.

Independence of Mind

Looking back on the foundation's improbable beginnings and
later success, I am reminded of what Yale College president
Timothy Dwight (1795–1817) often said about independence
of mind. It is a character trait often boasted of, he believed, but
rarely possessed and little understood.

"Probably there is nothing more frequently mistaken by our
race at large, or even by men of superior intelligence," as Dwight
himself put it. Most people believe themselves to be independent minded, because they are so ready to argue or to indulge a
passing mood. They foolishly equate the willingness to express
their emotions with the courage to follow one's calling, wherever
it leads.

True independence of mind, he wrote, is doing what one is
inspired to do in the wake of prayerful life, bounded by God's
moral law and uninhibited by what others say, is possible or

advantageous. It consists in living by St. Paul's famous injunction to the Thessalonian Christians: "Quench not the Spirit. Despise not prophesyings. Prove all things; hold fast that which is good."[69] (1 *Thessalonians* 5:19–21)

Like so many other early college presidents, Dwight learned this lesson from the survival of his own school. Long before the time when parents would sacrifice anything to get their children into Yale, Princeton, Stanford, or Duke—back when the viability of every American college was constantly threatened by economic crises, epidemics, natural disasters, and even wars—it was the president's faith in his own improbable vision which largely determined whether it would be realized.

If one insists on a modern technological metaphor for intuition, it makes a lot more sense to think of following the moment-by-moment driving directions appearing on a Google Maps app, set by God. No matter how unfamiliar the territory, how bad the traffic and weather conditions, how many wrong turns were previously taken, how critical the passengers are of one's driving, or how many unplanned stops had to be made, the next-step instruction is always the most reliable.

"That is the self which I would and do trust."

But how can we know for certain every intuition is, in fact, a Divine directive? May we not be tempted to confer spiritual legitimacy on some simmering resentment, coveted object, or lustful impulse by dressing it up in the guise of a higher calling?

Does not the *Bible* warn "the heart *is* deceitful above all *things*, and desperately wicked"? (*Jeremiah* 17:9) Does not Scripture also say, "out of the heart of men, proceed evil thoughts, adulteries, fornications, murders, thefts, covetousness, wickedness, deceit, lasciviousness, an evil eye, blasphemy, pride, foolishness"? (*Mark* 7:21–23)

How, then, can we know a seemingly inspired service is a Divine calling? May we not be mistaken? May we not interpret our own wishes as being His will?

Of course, we may be mistaken. Of course, we are tempted to misinterpret. That's one reason we were given the Ten Commandments—to help us separate a legitimate call from a seductive imposter.

As Case Western Reserve University president Charles F. Thwing (1890–1921) reminded his own students more than a century ago, "you can have no guide more true than…your best self: yourself instructed, calm in mood, strong to do the right, yourself reflective reverential…that is the self which I would and do trust…."[70] In other words, by keeping God present, praying daily for guidance, and observing His commandments, we separate out true spiritual promptings from whatever misguided impulses that could be mistaken for them.

If still in doubt, there is one more way to know that a seeming intuition is from God and that is simply to ask Him. Thwing's contemporary, Caroline Hazard (1899–1910), was president of one of America's first women's colleges, Wellesley, during the most turbulent period in that school's history. Enrollment had doubled, and the curriculum greatly expanded to include subjects previously taught only at men's colleges. Accommodating both these developments required costly and time-consuming renovations.

As much as Hazard believed in letting God intuitively guide her through these challenges, she often found herself juggling so many obligations and negotiating so many disagreements she wrote a special prayer to help her distinguish a real inspiration from the emotional noise. She called it her "Prayer for the Indwelling Spirit" and found it so helpful she often shared it during the school's chapel services. The Wellesley undergraduates found it so beneficial for themselves they memorialized the prayer in a 1903 book printed especially for alumnae:

> *"O, Love Divine, which was made flesh and dwelt among men, we come to thee with devout thanksgiving. Thou alone canst cleanse our hearts and make them a habitation for Thy indwelling spirit. Lord, Thou hast searched us. Thy word is quick and powerful. Thou knowest us altogether. May we open our hearts to Thee, the Divine Guest; not hiding in trembling fear, but throwing wide the door that Thou mayest enter, to cleanse, to purify, to enlarge, to fortify. Come to each soul in Thine own way, in the spoken word, in the sound of praise, in perfect silence; call us each by name, speak Thou in all our ministrations, that as we raise our hearts to Thee Thou wilt descend to us to fill us with Thine own Light and Peace, to dwell in us, the hope of glory. May we cast out whatever is impure or evil. Do Thou enter, O Lord, for in Thy presence is fullness of joy. So may we find true communion with Thee; so may we*

find pardon and newness of life; so may we become fit instruments of Thy praise. Amen.[71]

An abridged version, which Hazard found more convenient on the fly, went as follows:

Lord, Thou hast searched us. Thy word is quick and powerful. Thou knowest us altogether. May we open our hearts to Thee, the Divine Guest; not hiding in trembling fear, but throwing wide the door that Thou mayest enter, to cleanse, to purify to enlarge, to fortify.[72]

"Self-sacrifice Never Fails."

But what if, after doing all these things, one's heart is still divided? A choice presents itself, but how we intuitively feel about it changes from one hour to the next. It could be a seemingly minor decision, like how to spend an upcoming weekend off from work, or something as life changing as whether to accept a job offer in a city far across the country. But in either case, there is no consistently instinctive answer. The ancient Greeks had a word for this state, which literally translates into English as being "two spirited"—pulled in multiple directions or having stubbornly irreconcilable preferences.

It is easy to forget there is an added option to whatever we imagine our alternatives, and that is simply to do nothing for the moment. We should never rule out the possibility that what we are judging as "indecision" is really a spiritual directive to pause and seek out more information. Or at least to wait on further developments. Like the Biblical character Gideon, who was told by an angel he was chosen to liberate Israel from its oppressors but doubted his ability to do so, we may need further clarification as to what is being asked of us.

If waiting is indeed what is called for, the very consideration of that possibility tends to put the mind at ease. The great advantage of a spiritual outlook is we are not intimidated by ordinary time scales and know God's intentions frequently have little to do with what the material world considers urgent.

But what if, after listening to our inner voice, praying for clarity, trying to be a good person, and giving ourselves the option of inaction, we remain genuinely conflicted? Like Shakespeare's most famous character, Hamlet, we have the unrelenting sense something must be done. It is just not obvious what we are being called to do.

Christ could be said to have addressed the problem of unresolved ambiguity during the third day after his triumphal procession into Jerusalem. Speaking to an assembled crowd of priests, teachers, and elders, he famously laid out what he considered the two essential characteristics of the Christian life: "And thou shalt love the Lord thy God with all thy heart, and with all thy soul, and with all thy mind, and with all thy strength: this *is* the first commandment. And the second *is* like, *namely* this, Thou shalt love thy neighbour as thyself. There is none other commandment greater than these." (*Mark* 12:30–31)

We can easily take from this pronouncement when there is a persistent mystery over what action is being called for, the right course is the one that helps others most. Certainly, that is how the early college presidents interpreted the message.

"Self-sacrifice never fails" were always the parting words of Warren Akin Candler (1888–1898) to Emory College's graduating seniors. "Because self-sacrifice leads to a larger life, to a wider outlook, and to a more useful service, it has, by its very nature, the stamp of God's approval."[73]

"When in doubt [over] which of two courses to take, follow that which involves most self-denial," Mary Lyon (1837–1849) advised her own students at the Mt. Holyoke Female Seminary. "You will then find yourself in the safer and happier path, and walking with Him who denied himself for our sakes."[74] Yale University president Arthur Twining Hadley (1899–1921) readily agreed: "Each man finds his highest spiritual development, not by working out his own salvation alone and for himself, but by losing the thought of self in the thought of others."[75]

The great paradox, illustrated by the story of Temple University founder Russell Conwell (1887–1925), is that the sacrificial alternative almost always turns out to be a deeply self-satisfying one. Before he became Temple's first president, Conwell was a prosperous Philadelphia attorney who, despite his commercial success, found himself wrestling inconclusively with whether to expand his law firm or become a minister and then start a college.

Both inclinations felt "right," depending on the day of the week, but no sooner had he settled on one choice when the other would reassert itself. And because Conwell could always donate part of any increased legal income to good works, there were high-minded arguments for either course. Unable to make the decision intuitively, he finally decided to do what required the greater sacrifice of time and money.

Years later, when Conwell's biographer, Robert Shackleton, asked the Temple president how difficult it was to give up a lucrative profession to go into lower-paying academic work, Conwell answered with a twinkle in his eye. "Oh yes, it was a wrench," he admitted. But it was not long before the initial adjustment gave way to a strangely elevated feeling, what he called the "romance of self-sacrifice." And then he nodded to Shackleton with a smile, "I rather suppose the old-time martyrs rather enjoyed themselves in being martyrs."[76]

Scientific research in our own time has identified an intriguing phenomenon technically known as *hedonic adaptation*—which, in laymen's terms, means over time one's sense of material well-being returns to a baseline level, regardless of one's lifestyle. Winning the lottery, for example, will produce a temporary euphoria, just as being fired from a job leads to short-term depression. But over the long run, personal satisfaction has much more to do with the mood established by one's philosophy of life than by any change in physical circumstance. It follows then, self-sacrificial choices do not produce the feelings of deprivation the phrase *self-sacrifice* has come to imply.

Indeed, the decision to give up comfort for others can often produce some unexpected advantages, such as greater self-esteem and even an improvement in problem-solving skills. This is perhaps why an Australian study found that people who had to cope with the economic challenges of working in low-paying service jobs scored higher than average on tests of cognitive ability.[77]

There is an obvious limit to how far one can extrapolate from such scientific findings to the far grander problem of discerning God's will, but they do suggest the nature of self-sacrifice is sadly misunderstood in our time, even by many Christians. When it comes down to choosing between what is seemingly more pleasurable and what is spiritually prescribed, we must never forget God does a much better job of looking out for our well-being than we ever could.

The Good News about Robots

As I conclude this chapter on the importance of trusting intuition, I feel the need to say something about the rise of artificial intelligence, which many commentators have said will make human thought obsolete. Not a week goes by, it seems, without some new article by a supposed expert explaining why more and more Americans will soon have to yield to the superior wisdom of sophisticated machines.

Although this supposed threat to the employability of millions involves the convergence of multiple technologies—including computer programming, chip design, voice recognition, industrial automation, and material science—it is most often identified with the word *robot*, conjuring dark images of hapless workers callously sidelined by their faster, stronger, and smarter electronic rivals. The impression we are given is only slightly less grim than the impersonal future envisioned in Charlie Chaplin's classic silent film, *Modern Times*.

Political solutions to salvage what little dignity humans will supposedly have left are already being hotly debated. Those on the Left want a guaranteed income to pension off the growing number of workers they claim will be permanently displaced, while those on the Right demand school reforms to insure we do not fall too far behind our metallic rivals.

Yet there is a metaphysical aspect to the problem of artificial intelligence which, though I have not seen it discussed elsewhere, is deeply connected to a spiritual understanding of intuition. By metaphysical, I am simply referring to the fact that, for robots to even be considered a workplace threat, it must be assumed the complex tasks they perform are so like what a human being does their ascendency is only a matter of technological refinement.

But for someone who believes in a God who knows the future and will strategically intervene to insure his or her long-term well-being, robot technology represents nothing more than the same kind of challenge the automobile once did to the religious buggy whip salesman or the electric light bulb to the devout candlestick maker. It is certainly a good reason to pray for higher guidance in planning or changing one's career—and to be prepared for any temporary sacrifices such transitions might require—but hardly a reason to feel oneself obsolete or to believe the future will somehow be worse than the present.

People with a secular or materialistic view of what it means to be human have every reason to believe robots are a threat to their happiness. The kind of technology they fear may not have existed when James B. Angell was president of the University of Michigan (1871–1909), but his prediction that those who equate logical systems with true intelligence can never feel secure is as true today as it was a century ago.[78]

Those who believe in a transcendent soul and its relationship to God, on the other hand, are comforted by the knowledge that any similarity between persons and machines will never be more than a superficial one. Like one of the last of the old-time college presidents, Columbia University's Nicholas Murray Butler (1902–1945), they know the human mind has access to a wisdom far beyond anything ever to be programmed. It was for this reason, he often reminded his academic colleagues "not a few intellectual persons are quite unintelligent, and very many intelligent persons would hardly be classed as intellectual."[79]

Reflection:

*Trust in the LORD with all thine heart;
and lean not unto thine own understanding. In all thy
ways acknowledge him, and he shall direct thy paths.*
—Proverbs 3:5–6

BE NOT TOO WEDDED TO YOUR PLANS

God draweth straight lines but we call them crooked.

> —*Horace Mann, president of*
> *Antioch College (1853–1859)*[80]

A man who is over-anxious to accomplish specific results, however noble, who has fixed his whole heart thereon and his whole purpose therein, has fallen short of the full conception of the Christian life. "The kingdom of God cometh not with observation."

> —*Arthur Twining Hadley, president*
> *of Yale University (1899–1921)*[81]

Many a man fails in life because he is bent on acting upon some merely ideal plan, and is unwilling to work under actual conditions. This is rebellion

*against divine Providence, and argues pride and
selfishness, not nobility of purpose.*

—*Augustus Hopkins Strong, president of the
Rochester Theological Seminary (1872–1912)*[82]

"You can foretell nothing."

Noah Porter, who led Yale College from 1871 to 1886, often
challenged graduating seniors to draw a line in their minds
between the "clear and crowded" memories of their four previous years on campus and their expected careers which, no matter how eagerly anticipated, could never be envisioned with any
precision. "As you look forward to the future," he told them,
"it is hidden from your view by a curtain, beneath which and
through which you cannot look. In vain do you attempt even
to…outline the scenes that await you, to forecast the employ-
ments, the friends, the loves, the joys, the sorrows, the successes,
and the disappointments that are to make up your future. You
can discern nothing; you can foretell nothing."[83]

Porter's purpose was not to undermine his listeners' youthful
optimism, but to remind them the mental ability to model the
outside world and then devise strategies for engineering some
remote goal, while an excellent tool for serving God's purposes,
is also a limited one. The human mind, unaware of the universe
as He knows it, is incapable of either knowing or even roughly
modeling His intent; and so, while any inspiration to plan should
be obeyed, the projected outcome should never be idolized.

A popular anecdote in Porter's time told the story of the day when Saint Francis of Assisi, the famous thirteenth century Italian friar, agreed to instruct a novice monk in how to preach the Gospel. Early one morning he led the young cleric out of town to begin the lesson, but no sooner had the two set out when they were interrupted by a farmer whose cart was broken down, requiring them to stop and help.

Later that morning, they came across a despondent merchant and politely paused to let him share his troubles. And no sooner had the merchant finished, when the monks found themselves sharing their food with some hungry beggars passing by. After lunch, they prayed with a sick woman on the road and on their way back home, helped another woman carry a heavy load.

It was not until after dark when the disappointed novice finally accompanied Francis back to the monastery. The entire day went by, he noted sadly, but they had not preached to anyone. "To the contrary, my son," Francis corrected him, "we've been sharing the Gospel at every turn."

Not every human plan is so quickly or abruptly disrupted, Porter assured his undergraduates, but if history proved anything, it was that even the most rigorously pursued course will have an outcome very different than originally conceived. The ancient alchemists never did realize their dream of turning lead into gold, but their failure inadvertently led to something far more valuable—the scientific method of doing research. Thomas Jefferson's plan to have explorers Lewis and Clark scout the contours of a separate country in the Northwest he wanted to call "the Republic of Cascadia" had the very opposite effect of vastly expanding the United States. As confident as he was his well-trained army of 680,000 men could subdue Russia, the French Emperor Napoleon had not counted on the winter weather which eventually defeated him.

For Porter, nothing better demonstrated the inherent inaccuracy of any humanly conceived plan than the story of the first Puritan settlers and their attempt to establish a religious community in North America. As it turned out, all their advance estimations about where to best locate a colony, what crops to grow, how to get along with the indigenous peoples, and how to coexist with the commercial settlements that would likely follow turned out to be wildly inaccurate. And certainly nothing in the Puritans' mission gave any hint of the kind of country their efforts would eventually give birth to: a nation whose personal, social, and political values they could scarcely grasp.

All this did not mean the Puritan founders should never have sailed from Europe in the first place, Porter was quick to add. But God's interest in promoting the venture clearly had less to do with faithfully executing the colonists' preconceived plan than with the many unforeseeable detours which occurred along the way.

"We had no suspicion of their importance."

The spiritual discipline of not becoming overly attached to one's plans means, first, having the flexibility to invest time in those inconvenient, irrelevant, or seemingly trivial intuitions nevertheless tinged with an inexplicable sense of urgency. In other words, do not dismiss an interest or inspiration that knocks loudly on the door of consciousness simply because it seems to interfere with more important pursuits, makes no obvious sense, or would be dismissed by others as a waste of time.

Looking back on his life and career, another Yale College president, Theodore Woolsey (1846–1871), often spoke of how tangential interests, given some room to grow, become critical "turning points in our lives, [even] when we had no suspicion of their importance." All "who have passed the boundaries of youth can testify that an unexpected future has been unrolling itself before us through all our years," he wrote in *The Religion of the Present and of the Future.* We are blessed when we realize that novel digressions, "wholly unforeseen," often represent God's intervention in "the times and seasons of human life." And we should therefore give them room to develop, however difficult this may be to logically justify.[84]

As annoyingly inconvenient as our spiritual diversions may sometimes seem, Princeton's James McCosh (1868–1888) told his students, the flexible person will "discover that God has led him in a wonderful way [which, though he did not wish it at the time] he now sees to be full of wisdom, turning him aside when he was entering upon a dangerous path and opening a road for his relief when he was shut in, restraining him when he was advancing too rapidly, and stimulating him when he was becoming slothful and discouraged."[85]

Emory University chancellor Warren Akin Candler (1888–1898) was even more emphatic. When taken with a problem that seems to have no relevance to your ambitions, he said, that is the most important time to remember God's ever-presence. "Do not be so ready to presume that the Holy Spirit is talking to someone else. He is talking to you."[86]

Among the early college presidents, few provided a better example of honoring "nonsensical" callings than Philip Lindsley (1824–1850). Born in 1786 in Basking Ridge, New Jersey, he attended the College of New Jersey (before it was renamed Princeton), where he was such an outstanding student, he was asked to stay on to teach both Latin and Greek. By 1813, he became a Professor of Languages, college Dean, and Secretary to the Board of Trustees—all rolled into one person. And when he was appointed Princeton's Acting President in 1822, it was just assumed he would either stay on or take over some other prestigious school.

That was Lindsley's plan as well, but at the very moment he was receiving offers from prominent institutions throughout the country, he found himself inexplicably possessed by the idea of growing a small college in a relatively remote part of the country. His friends and family openly worried Lindsley had gone mad, but when he was asked to assume the presidency of tiny Cumberland College in Nashville, Tennessee, he promptly agreed. His only condition was the school's name be ambitiously changed to the University of Nashville.

As time went on, there were days when Lindsley must have doubted his own sanity for it seems the state legislature was never really prepared to fund a major university in Nashville. By 1850, the school was forced to suspend operations for five years because of a cholera epidemic that devastated enrollment, strained finances, and finally caused it to fail.

And yet looking back on his career, Lindsley could take great satisfaction in knowing even his limited success in Tennessee was enough to inspire the founding of colleges and universities throughout the South. When he originally agreed to take over Cumberland College in 1824, there was no similar school for over two hundred miles in any direction—not in Alabama, Arkansas, Louisiana, Mississippi, Texas, or elsewhere in Tennessee. But by 1855, there were more than thirty, nine within fifty miles of Nashville alone.[87]

Lindsley, it turned out, was not such a fool to follow his "foolish" intuition back at Princeton, even if the ultimate purpose for which he was guided was never made clear to him. When making decisions, he came to see, it is God's plans and not any calculation of our own to which we must "humbly and devoutly" defer. "To the infinite Fountain of grace and wisdom I must continually look—to the Eternal Giver of every good and perfect gift we must all look, for that support and direction which we so eminently need."[88]

If what passes for wisdom in our own time has yet to recover the spiritual insight of the early college presidents, there is at least a growing recognition among contemporary psychologists that doing what seems to be logical is not always very smart. A 2012 study by Richard West at James Madison University and Keith Stanovich at the University of Toronto, for example, found people with high IQs are often more vulnerable to making bad mistakes than their supposedly less gifted neighbors. Precisely because they assume their intelligence gives them an automatic edge, they tend to overestimate how much they really know about a situation, what is required to deal with it, and what unconscious attachments they may have to unworkable solutions.[89]

In researching their book on *The Greatest Business Decisions of All Time*, Verne Harnish and his colleagues at *Fortune* magazine found almost every instance of exceptional commercial success involved a CEO who departed so radically from the company's previous practices that both colleagues and competitors considered the move rash. This was as true of Henry Ford's abrupt decision to double his employees' salaries as it was of Boeing president Bill Allen's 1954 choice to build a commercial airliner without a single order in hand. Or, for that matter, the willingness of Apple's board in 1997 to rehire its once-fired founder, Steve Jobs.

"True work, divinely appointed, is never lost."

Of course, it is one thing to depart from one's path when the digression is temporary or the abandoned plan is relatively new, quite another when considerable time and money have already been invested toward a particular goal. It is at those times when an intuitive call seems especially inconvenient or disruptive, we must remember God's capacity for weaving together many seemingly disconnected and unrelated strands. In other words, the fact that longstanding efforts have not come to fruition does not mean they have served no useful purpose.

"True work, divinely appointed, is never lost…," Dartmouth College president Asa D. Smith (1863–1866) constantly reassured his students. "It may seem to have vanished…it may be hidden from the eyes of men; there may be no earthly revelation or glorification of the worker. But God shall take care of it. It is the precious grain that shall never fail; and when the hand that sowed it is moldering in the dust, it shall bring forth thirty, sixty, or a hundred-fold."[90]

Williams College president Mark Hopkins (1836–1872) liked to tell his undergraduates the story of how he started out in life studying medicine, fully intending to set up a practice in New York City. No job could have been further from his mind when he read of an opening to teach moral philosophy and public speaking at a small Massachusetts school, but a voice in the back of his head told him to pack away his physician's textbooks, read up as quickly as he could on the subjects mentioned in the notice, and apply for the position.

It was not until some years after Hopkins had convinced the Williams faculty to take a chance on hiring a doctor for a professor's job, when the college's president unexpectedly resigned. Normally Hopkins would have been considered far too young and inexperienced to be considered as a replacement, but the fact he mastered subjects as diverse as medicine, moral philosophy, and public speaking could not be ignored. So, when that year's graduating class submitted a letter to the board of trustees, expressing unanimous gratitude for the privilege of having studied under such a broadly educated person, the possibility of his appointment at least had to be considered.

"If the boys want him," one of the trustees finally said, "let them have him." And that was how New York City's shortest serving physician, who made an improbably abrupt turn to the ministry, ended up in a job that would allow Hopkins to become one of the most influential educators in American history.[91]

While giving hundreds of talks across the United States on the connection between spiritual values and emotional health, I have met many people who told me stories of the gifts unexpectedly cycled back to them from an abandoned course, in which they were once heavily invested. Having had the courage to follow their spiritual intuitions through a sequence of seemingly disconnected life events, they arrived at a place where they could look back on all the twists and turns to recognize an intelligent pattern they could never have consciously constructed. Not all would say living intuitively made for easy or comfortable decisions, but they would agree that leaving a part of one's life behind is not the same thing as wasting the energy invested in it. (Likely this is what former US President Dwight Eisenhower meant to convey when he cryptically observed "planning is indispensable" but "plans are useless."[92])

One man I met was a former Hollywood actor who, after a long career as a supporting player in low-budget science-fiction movies, suddenly felt called to study for the ministry. Not long after receiving his master's degree, his wife declared she was no longer happy living in Los Angeles; so they moved to Texas, where he was asked to be the pastor of a small church. By the time I was first introduced to him, the former actor's congregation had grown to one of the largest in the Dallas area—a development he attributed in part to the speaking skills he developed in front of movie cameras.

Then there was the case of a woman who grew up in a poor family on the outskirts of Fairfield County, one of the most affluent areas in Connecticut. Unable to afford college, she started working as an au pair in the nearby upscale town of Darien and because she was so personable, began to receive more promising job offers in the community. No sooner had she saved a little money than her initial desire to achieve a comfortable suburban lifestyle was unexpectedly replaced by the impulse to travel. Applying for a series of positions widely separated geographically, she eventually became custodian for a New Mexico art gallery, where after hours she could indulge an even newer passion to paint.

By the time I met her, the woman was happily running her own talent agency in Santa Fe, representing herself and other local artists. As we talked, she confided it was the experience of babysitting for affluent families which, more than anything else, gave her the confidence she needed to work with the kind of people wealthy enough to invest in art.

Certainly, one of the most interesting characters I ever met was an attorney who, as a younger man starting his own practice, had enough free time to become fascinated with a very unusual kind of title search. Instead of tracing property lines from the present backwards (which is how it is normally done), he experimented with doing the opposite. He located museum-preserved copies of land grants from the King of England to the first American colonists and then traced the ownership forward.

It was an engaging hobby he devoted considerable time to, but as both his workload and family grew larger, the attorney finally decided to give it up. It was not until over a decade later, when a client came to him for help in resolving a property dispute with a neighbor, the lawyer remembered the one thing which most surprised him about following title changes from past to present. By doing so, it is possible to identify boundary changes which are not obvious when searching the conventional way.

It then occurred to the attorney his earlier experience with past-to-present title searching, combined with what he learned since from practicing law, might enable him to help people who are the unknowing heirs of valuable properties once owned by distant ancestors—properties whose plot plans had been wrongfully altered in the past and then sold to, or claimed by, water utilities, agricultural businesses, and real estate developers. In just a few short years, he went on to create a successful business identifying fraudulently appropriated land lots and returning them to their rightful holders. And it was all possible because of a hobby he was once heavily invested in but was guided to abandon.

Mass Miseducation

If the early college presidents were alive today, they would undoubtedly be alarmed by two contemporary developments. The first is the evolution of a childrearing culture which elevates the importance of attending an elite college by satisfying very narrow admissions requirements: great grades, high scores on national tests, school leadership positions, and some kind impressive-sounding community service.

If living spiritually in the material world requires the ability to detach from plans that no longer resonate with one's inner voice, America's current educational system is almost diabolically designed to promote the opposite: the dogged pursuit of specific accomplishments which, if realized, will presumably enchant the rest of one's life. In her book *The Price of Privilege*, adolescent psychologist Madeline Levine describes in depressing detail how so many of today's students are taught from a very young age precisely what hoops they must jump through to land on a desirable campus, faking enthusiasms they lack while failing to pursue genuine interests less likely to impress a college admissions officer.

Today's students are made to understand very clearly what is required to get into a good college, Levine writes, but not how to be faithful to their inner voices. From their earliest years, they are busily chauffeured from one activity to the next, gathering ever-more impressive credentials, but at the same time learning to mistrust what they are intuitively drawn to.

The early college presidents would hardly be surprised by statistics showing 17 percent of today's undergraduates have been diagnosed with severe anxiety and 13.9 percent with depression.[93] How, after all, is it possible for a young person who has never been encouraged to cultivate his or her spiritual sense of direction to have genuine self-confidence—to believe, as Yale's Noah Porter (1871–1886) once put it, "He who has brought you to this place" will direct you wisely "to the end"?[94] Ill-equipped to make internally grounded decisions, they become susceptible to unhealthy peer pressures and the temptation to numb their underlying sense of self-betrayal with mood-altering drugs.

Even those who do make it through college relatively unscathed end up settling for unrewarding jobs and relationships. Having been conditioned since childhood to plod dependably toward some well-defined path, they habitually reject more intriguing alternatives, which almost by definition are outside the mainstream. About the best they can do is mimic the language or dress of some popular hero—the director of a ground-breaking film, the inventor of some high-tech gadget, or perhaps a political activist—never thinking the person being imitated is widely esteemed precisely because he or she has not been imitating anyone else.

The Worldly Technology of Spiritual Growth

Had the early college presidents somehow survived our time, they would also be concerned about another modern dysfunction: the failure to clarify the social conventions which, in past times, made it possible for a responsible person to be available to the unfamiliar, the unconventional, or seemingly impractical without, at the same time, creating unfair chaos in the lives of others. It is the failure to spiritually define the meaning of two still commonly used, but widely misunderstood, words: *contract* and *commitment*.

Consider for a moment the case of a man we'll call Fred. He lives in a comfortable suburban home he wants to make even more attractive by clearing a wooded area behind his house. Specifically, he wants to tear down some ugly trees and the poison ivy running up and down them, as well as pull up the thorny raspberry bushes nearby. In their place, he wants to plant grass and dig a fire pit for summer cookouts.

So, Fred draws up a rough plan of how big a space he needs to clear, along with a sketch of how the grill should look and where on the lawn it should be sited. Then he calls in a couple of landscapers to get estimates for doing the job and perhaps a sense of how he feels about working with each. Finally, Fred signs an agreement with one of the landscapers which details a work schedule, the prices of both material and labor, the required down payment, and the balance due when the job is finished.

Now, as contracts go, this is a relatively simple one. If, instead, Fred were the CEO of a large company interested in building a new factory, the agreement would be far more complex and likely involve multiple contractors or subcontractors. And yet all contracts tend to have one very important quality in common: they are time limited. Even the largest construction projects are brought to completion as quickly as possible, just as are agreements to start or sell a business, commission works of art, or repair a damaged car. The most complicated special effects movie, involving hundreds of cast and crew, still finishes principal production within just months.

If asked why this is so, most people today would likely give some very sensible sounding reasons:

- The quicker the project is done, the less it will cost
- By agreeing to work on a clearly-defined schedule, the contractor can safely book other jobs
- Because the price of materials needed to complete almost any project can change over time, it is better to finish while the budget can be accurately calculated
- And, most practical of all, the sooner the deal is done, the sooner the finished product can be put to use, be it a barbeque pit, a factory, or a movie

But, as the early college presidents long ago recognized, there is another, more spiritual reason why every contract should be time limited. God's will for each person changes with time, and therefore no one should make a binding agreement too far into the future—or, conversely, claim the right to another's labor beyond that same point. That is why Scripture tells us, on the one hand, "a man diligent in his business…shall stand before kings" (*Proverbs* 22:29). And yet, when Jesus said to Peter and his companions, "Follow me, and I will make you fishers of men," they are right to drop their nets and join Him. (*Matthew* 4:19)

On their surface, modern legal codes would seem to reflect little interest in the spiritual dimension of labor, but wisely neither do they contradict it. US courts have inherited a tradition of voiding contracts simply because the terms were unreasonably long or binding. And, while the original religious reasoning for this has long been forgotten, there remains a legal tradition that every person, no matter his skills, background, social status, or reputation, has the right to change direction over time without justifying the move to anyone but himself. Sadly, few people today could cite the origins of this right and therefore have difficulty understanding how one can be both spiritual and socially responsible.

"But aren't there some agreements we should want to think of as lifelong?" I can imagine some readers objecting. The decision to marry for example, or the obligations of parents to their children?

This brings us to the second commonly misunderstood word, *commitment*. It, too, is a contract of sorts, but one which keeps the soul free to serve God, not with minimal terms, but by so intertwining one believer's life with another's they become (as wedding vows used to stress) a unity. And "the two shall become one flesh," it says in *Mark* 10:8, thereby able to serve His purposes in ways not possible apart.

Some clergy make this kind of contract when they pledge their loyalty to the church above all else. Down through history, elite warriors have also made such pacts, either amongst themselves or with their sovereign. But for the overwhelming bulk of the world's population, it is the commitment to marriage and family which provides the spiritual opportunity to bind on Earth with another soul.

An unfortunate side effect of technological progress has been to obscure the value of this commitment by rendering its benefits less materially obvious. Unlike earlier times, when each spouse clearly gained from a clear division of labor—one out in the working world, the other tending the hearth—modern conveniences have now made it possible for both to have independent careers. And while this is genuine progress, there are inevitable strains whenever one partner is presented with a career opportunity that seems to call for the other to sacrifice.

From the limited perspective of calculable gains and losses, the cumulation of such challenges can even create the impression the marriage itself is the problem, forcing both spouses to make too many unwanted compromises. Without the spiritual understanding that the "we" gives rise to something much greater than whatever material sacrifices are required to preserve it, the resentment of one or both parties can produce a relationship-destroying cycle of anger and withdrawal.

What we have unfortunately lost today is the once obvious understanding that, when two people commit to each other by way of a shared faith, an extraordinarily powerful vehicle is created for the expression of God's will on Earth. Both partners become not merely two new creatures, but a superior being in whom the appearance of sacrifice is but a measure of its greatness.[95]

As the presidents liked to quote from *Romans* 8:28, "...we know that all things work together for good to them that love God, to them who are the called according to *his* purpose." Or in the more contemporary words of Christian psychiatrist Thomas Hora, "When a marriage is based on joint participation in the good of God, the quality of happiness and well-being is entirely different from moments of pleasure based on ego-gratification. Ego-gratification is exciting and pleasurable, 'heady.' [But] this is counterfeit happiness; it is short-lived and has an obverse side of pain and disappointment. If in a situation there is an awareness of the good of God, which is spiritual blissfulness characterized by peace, assurance, gratitude, and love—then we are on the right track."[96]

A spiritual commitment is not an agreement to divvy out equal pleasures or property; nor is it a mere checklist of expectations. It is a contract where the most beautiful, most harmonious, and most intelligent earthly life can be realized. It is a relationship, not just with each other, but with God.

Docility of the Heart

Single or married, we are always making the most progress whenever we give a higher priority to spiritual intuition than to a preconceived goal, whenever we become more eager to serve God than to execute an existing plan. "Docility of heart," as Amherst

College president Julius H. Seelye (1876–1890) once put it
man's priceless endowment, and should be his perpetual p
sion…. Only thus do we come into true communion with
who came not to be ministered unto, but to minister, and
in becoming a servant showed Himself to be lord of all."[97]

The willingness to temporarily divert from, or even
don, one's course is not the invitation to chaos we are taug
imagine. Nor is it giving oneself permission to be blindly in
sive. The readiness to go where called is simply a recogniti
the fact that how a person organizes his or her life is less im
ant than Who it is lived for.

If a young child needs the guidance of a wise teach
begin the process of becoming an educated person—if som
entering college should sit down with a faculty advisor to
clearer idea of the school's curriculum—if someone just ente
a trade or profession is wise to seek out an experienced r
tor—how much more must every person need to be attune
the promptings of the wisest being of all? A mere human ca
more anticipate the best way to act in the months or years a
than he or she could, at any moment, comprehend the w
mechanism of the universe.

Reflection:

*…Consider the lilies of the field, how they grow;
they toil not, neither do they spin: And yet I say unto you,
That even Solomon in all his glory was not arrayed like
one of these. Wherefore, if God so clothe the grass of the
field, which today is, and tomorrow is cast into the oven,
shall he not much more clothe you, O ye of little faith?*
—Matthew 6:28–30

DO NOT SUCCUMB TO SOFT ATHEISM

Thus it is that while there are very few avowed atheists in the world, there are many real ones; while there are few in word there are many in deed.... And we pray for you to consider how fearful is your condition if, instead of being almost Christians, as some of you may hope you are, you shall be found to be far from God and hope....

—Rev. Lewis W. Green, president of Hampden–Sydney College (1848–1856)[98]

Do what today calls for; fill it with everything which it asks; make such preparations for the future as the work which is under your care demands and the probabilities of continued life suggest as wise. But be content when you have done this. Do not hinder the efficiency of today by anxiety for tomorrow. Do not make the uncertainty of results which you cannot control a burden upon your soul. That this plan is the right one for limited beings like ourselves can scarcely be doubted. That it is a reasonable one is certain when we observe the facts of our earthly life. But for peacefulness it is the only plan. The man who makes it his rule to do the utmost that he can and ought to do today, and waits calmly for tomorrow...must be undisturbed.

—*Timothy Dwight V, president of Yale University (1886–1899)*[99]

We think of things of which we ought not to think. We often make ourselves unhappy by dwelling on our condition and prospects, and those of our friends. But it is our blessed privilege to commit all these to Him, who will certainly take care of us, if He sees we are not afraid to trust Him. What a wonder that the Infinite God is willing to take thought for us, and it is a greater wonder that we are not willing to trust him. With God to take thought for us, we need never [worry].

—*Mary Lyon, president of Mt. Holyoke Female Seminary (1837–1849)*[100]

The Burden of Contingency Planning

Attempting to accomplish anything we value requires us to make reasonable provision for how we might be thwarted by unfavorable or unexpected developments. No matter how beautiful the outdoor setting the couple has chosen for their wedding, for example, there should always be a sheltered alternative close by in case of rain. And while no one ever buys a car with the intention of smashing it up, having accident insurance is also a good idea. Even going out to a favorite restaurant suggests a backup plan, if the place does not take reservations.

A certain amount of remedial anticipation—"contingency planning," modern organization experts call it—often makes sense, even when the probability of needing a fallback is low. But how much and at what cost?

Think of how much anticipatory speculation the modern family must do each time a new job or promotion calls for moving to a new town. With every house or rental seen, consideration must be given to the quality of local schools, the seeming direction of real estate values, access to medical care, overdue maintenance on the residence, the price of home insurance, and so on. Given that the average American family moves at least twelve times for work or some other reason[101], that is a lot of contingency planning just to keep a roof over everyone's head.

The anticipation required to avoid, or at least to manage, possible negative consequences suggests an interesting paradox. For does there not come a point where the time and effort exhausted in insuring against a failure or a setback become more of a burden than the failure or setback one has been seeking to avoid?

Take the not uncommon case of the young man who feels called to an artistic career but, fearing it might not work out, spends most of his early twenties preparing for a second and more practical vocation—one whose chances of success he can more confidently depend upon if the first choice does not work out. The budding novelist might decide to get a teaching certificate, for example, so he or she can have "something to fall back on" in case his stories do not sell as well as hoped. The effective attitude is, "Sure, I'll go where the Spirit leads me. But before I start, I just want to be sure I've constructed a realistic safety net."

But what kind of security is it really? When contingency planning has gotten to the point of spending two years in some graduate school of education, cramming to pass the state exam, and piling up considerable student debt in the process, who has time to write?

Does this mean, if the would-be novelist were to focus more on storytelling—adding as much time to sitting in front of the word processor as he or she would have spent preparing a fall-back—one's literary success is assured? Of course not. Talent does not always match ambition; and, after a few years of dedicated effort with unpromising results, it could well become evident one's fictional skills are more limited than originally hoped.

But if we think about it, the probability of imagined success is not the real issue. The important question is not whether a heartfelt desire always leads to the hoped-for result, but whether a loving God would ask His devoted servant to try and write stories unless it served a useful purpose—perhaps preparation for a related occupation, such as journalism or editorial work. For if one is guided by an intuitive sense of God's will, failing is never failing; it is just the end of a phase in a life whose spiritual purpose is not yet visible. This is what Emory College president Atticus Greene Haygood (1876–1884) was trying to impress

upon his school's graduating seniors when he promised them, "One thing is for sure—there is a place [in God's plan] for you if you are only fit for it; or there will be when you become fit."[102]

And if we think about it a little more, the very idea of a fallback career is really a soft form of atheism. For in the end, what is the difference between excessive caution and an absence of faith in the calling of a present God?

To believe in an all-powerful God is to believe He is here and now, with all His attributes and powers, ready to direct our affairs far more effectively than we could possibly do it ourselves.[103] To act as if we must preserve a more secure alternative to our present course betrays a very different belief: we do not believe God is acting in our daily lives, we do not acknowledge His Spirit pervading our minds and hearts, we do not have faith in His justice and fairness, and we do not believe He coordinates all things for an ultimate good, which includes our own.

It means, in other words, we have completely missed what Jesus meant when he said: "I am with you always, *even* unto the end of the world." (*Matthew* 28:20)[104]

Imprudent Prudence

The spiritual danger of being too cautious was fundamental to the teachings of America's early college presidents. There "is a kind of prudence, falsely so called," Dartmouth University president Asa Dodge Smith (1863–1866) wrote to a student, "which exerts a pernicious influence on the cause of Christ." A person, he added, "who gets into the habit of inquiring about proprieties and expediencies and occasions often spends his life without doing anything to purpose."[105]

Smith's contemporary, Duke University president Braxton Craven (1842–1863), gave very similar advice each year in his annual sermon to the school's graduating seniors: "Much of the world's misery, poverty and shame arises from wrong pursuits; much of the ridiculous folly and fantastic vanity of every day's occurrence is but the surging of souls capable of great things, but have missed the orbit of life. Talented men fail by the thousand, because God is angry at their disobedience...."[106]

Conversely, Craven promised, there is in every man or woman "an undying inclination, which is the voice of God proclaiming your mission. If you gird yourself in the bonds of strength and move at this Divine bidding, the arm of Jehovah will be around you, Jesus will watch you from the mercy seat, angels shall be your ministers and arch-angels your guardians."[107]

This is admittedly flowery language by contemporary standards, but the wisdom it expresses was the same advice the presidents preached to themselves when called upon to serve God in ways that, from a practical viewpoint, seemed unlikely to succeed. Take Booker T. Washington, best remembered today as the freed slave who, in 1881, founded the Tuskegee Institute and went on to become the most famous African American leader of the late nineteenth and early twentieth centuries.

Less well-remembered is just how difficult it was to finance and sustain the deep South's first all-black college in the years immediately following the Civil War. Money for anything, let alone construction materials for a new campus or scholarships for poor students, was scarce, with the result Washington had to mobilize volunteers to cook food and erect campus facilities—all the while staving off an occasional lynch mob of disgruntled Confederates. When people asked him why the Institute taught farming alongside history, math, and classical literature, his answer was simple, "Because we wanted something to eat."[108]

As his fame grew and Washington was increasingly offered more financially-secure opportunities to teach and write, he never wavered in his commitment to the Institute, which he continued to feel was his God-given work. Indeed, he never accepted a lecture invitation unless the topic in some way promoted his school.[109]

So convinced were the early college presidents of the need to avoid hedging one's spiritual calling that Case Western Reserve president Charles F. Thwing (1890–1921) thought up an experiment to prove it. Inspired by the fact his own son was about to go to college, he decided to study the careers of Case's graduates with an eye toward identifying those qualities which best predicted their later success. His subjects included lawyers, editors, judges, and clergymen as well as teachers, merchants, manufacturers, and architects.

Family background and connections proved helpful in landing a recent graduate his first job, Thwing was not surprised to discover, but had surprisingly little influence over the longer run. Sociability also turned out to have little effect. Some of Case's most respected graduates had outgoing personalities, but others remained shy and modest throughout their lives.

"I will not say that [the most accomplished] men did the best he could at every step of the way," Thwing finally reported. "Some did, some did not probably." But what they did have in common was "that each did better than the place demanded." In other words, their energies were focused on their chosen work, not depleted by efforts to create an insurance policy against failing at what they really wanted to do.[110]

Modern career experts may rarely cite early college presidents like Thwing, but a spiritual truth has a way of suggesting itself regardless of professional lexicon. When recently asked by the business cable network CNBC why some people are more successful than others, for example, bestselling management guru Suzy Welch didn't skip a beat. It can be explained in just six words, she said: "Successful people have no plan B."[111]

Soft Atheism II

An excessive investment in career fallbacks is a very common form of soft atheism, but not the only one. Something similar happens when, looking down the road at what our calling seems to require and seeing so many obstacles to be overcome, we allow ourselves to feel overwhelmed by the imagined effort. "This can't be what God wants!" we say to ourselves. "This is just some fantasy, really a daydream. Surely it would be better to wait until something more manageable comes along."

Consider the woman who is taken with the desire to become a nurse practitioner but has not studied all the college courses needed to apply for admission to an accredited graduate program. How, with her current job and responsibilities, can she find the time to make up the required subjects? Where will she get the money? What will it feel like to no longer have any free time, perhaps for years to come? The more she dwells on the difficulty of the task, the more her resolution waivers.

Or take the case of the man who has been sufficiently disturbed by press reports of corruption in city hall that he feels called upon to run for local office as a reformer. He has a business background and so a good idea of how to straighten out the town's finances; but almost immediately, his friends remind him politics can be a dirty business. Those who profit from the current dysfunction will almost certainly attack him personally, they say. Neighbors will turn on him simply because they belong to a different political party. The more he reflects on these downsides, the more the seeming sacrifices required erode his civic impulse.

The point here is not to deny the would-be nurse's or aspiring politician's imagined obstacles. But it should never be forgotten that every Divinely-inspired act links us to a network of other Divinely-inspired actors, such that any challenging demonstration of our faith mobilizes unforeseen allies on its behalf—not only friends and acquaintances, but sometimes even complete strangers who, at just the right moment, step in to lift some of the burden from our shoulders. If our intentions only went as far as we could see, as Duke's Craven once put it, we might be justified in questioning our prospects, but "our gardens bear herbs we never planted, a strange hand hath grafted all our trees, and every day there is a guest at our table we never invited."[112]

Yale president Timothy Dwight V (1886–1899) was not as poetic as Craven but spoke for all the early college presidents when he observed the longer faithful Christians live, the more they come to see how a spiritually-inspired mission invariably

surmounts the obstacles in front of it, although often in round-
about and unexpected ways. If a man "has been working for a
score or two of years," Dwight wrote, "[and if] he has grown
older in the way in which God would have him grow, he has
become trustful in God's wisdom...."[113]

Mary Lyon (1837–1849), who quit a secure job during the
1834 economic depression to found the Mount Holyoke Female
Seminary, knew from her own experience that "we have only to
go on and do present duty, and God will take care of the future."
One thought "often overwhelms me," she confided to her students after the school opened its doors in 1837. "God, the great
God, taking care of me and willing to let me trust him! If all is
dark—if there is universal darkness, and long continued—we
may still trust God, if we are willing to obey him. If you are
Christ's, do not seek for certainty and security in this life. Jesus
never led one of his children in that way. We must trust him."[114]

In 1922, retired University of Denver chancellor William
Fraser McDowell (1890–1899) wrote a book, in which he
recalled going to church as a child in Millersburg, Ohio. There
was no lack of joyful worship, he said, but never about expressing God's will, which always seemed to be darkly associated with
notions of suffering, sacrifice, and harsh discipline.

It was not until years later, while supervising an expansion
of the university's campus, when he discovered for himself the
extent to which following God's will has the effect of inspiring
others to help. "We have inherited a miserable idea that the will
of God is to be suffered or endured," he concluded, "that it is
hard and grinding, that it finds its chief expression in afflictions,

personal trials, and disagreeable duties, especially forcing choice youth into unattractive occupations."[115]

The right attitude toward one's calling, McDowell went on, is "wherever, whenever, whatever He wants, I am for it, for it is the best thing going." It is when we can almost imagine Jesus saying enthusiastically "Come, let us do this or that, let us go here or there" unexpected forces become mobilized to clear our path.[116]

Coming down to our own time, we have the countless testimonies of Christians who say the most important lesson they ever learned was mustering the courage to do what they sensed they were being called to do, regardless of any fears or imagined difficulties. In a 2017 interview with the *Washington Post*, Yale University neuroscientist Jaime Maldonado-Aviles expressed this very sentiment with respect to his recent decision to leave a successful scientific career to study for the priesthood. Having once before experienced the forces that come to the aid of a difficult calling—his childhood determination to go from Puerto Rico to the Ivy League—he was no longer worried about anticipated obstacles to his new sense of direction. "If I believe God is calling me to be a priest," he told the reporter, "I also believe He will give me charisms—the gifts—that will help me."[117]

Perhaps the most famous example of this outlook was Walt Disney, who as a boy had already developed the habit of following what he believed to be a higher calling, regardless of the consequences. "I believe firmly in the efficacy of religion, in its powerful influence on a person's whole life," he wrote in a 1949 cover article for *Guideposts* magazine. "It helps immeasurably to meet the storm and stress of life and keep you attuned to the Divine inspiration.... All I ask of myself, 'Live a good Christian life.' To that objective I bend every effort in shaping my personal, domestic, and professional activities and growth."[118]

Such advice undoubtedly sounds hokey to many a modern ear. But as secular as society has become, there is almost universal agreement among policymakers that any social program tends to work better if it can be delegated to a religious organization. Whether the goal is to provide affordable housing to the poor, halt an urban drug epidemic, or offer preschool programs for minority children, public services tend to be more successful when run by church groups, either independently or in partnership with businesses or government agencies. Religious skeptics may not like to acknowledge it, but the quality the spiritually motivated person brings to his or her work is clearly the difference which so often makes the biggest difference.[119]

Soft Atheism III

The third and final form of soft atheism occurs when we do muster the courage to follow our spiritual intuition but take it upon ourselves to judge what constitutes an acceptable rate of progress. We are not content to "run with patience the race that is set before us" (*Hebrews* 12:1) and leave to God the proper evaluation of what has been accomplished.

There is an old saying to the effect that faith "is waiting on God's time without doubting God's truth." The early college presidents believed it was more accurate to say faith is waiting on God's *training* without doubting God's truth. As University of Wisconsin president John Bascom (1874–1887) liked to say, "Waiting is not waiting" but something more akin to the breaking of a wild horse. It is "the curbing of our superficial and fitful thoughts" until they better conform to "the unfolding purposes and sustaining love of our Heavenly Father."[120]

Oberlin's Henry Churchill King (1902–1927) clearly agreed. The true believer, he once put it, "knows that both man's nature and the Christian ideal call him to endless growth…. At every stage, he knows well that he faces [the] task of rising above his circumstances and not being ruled by them."[121]

Patience, King believed, is really just another word for depending on God. Like the wise farmer in *James* 5:7–20, who knows a good crop requires both "the early and latter rain," a truly religious person does not try to skip the intervening events required for the perfection of God's harvest.

Carl Jung, the most famous twentieth century psychotherapist to oppose the rise of psychological materialism, was so convinced of what the early college presidents had said about patience he automatically gave the name *God* to anything that held him back—including, as he put it, "all things which upset my subjective views, plans and intentions and change the course of my life, for better or worse."[122] Genuine achievement, Jung explained to his patients, rests on the ability to accept the renovating forces of the world and, by so doing, grow into the Divine mind. What so often seems little more to our "mole-like vision" than fruitlessly flinging ourselves against unbreakable walls is, in fact, a necessary aspect of spiritual progress.

In truth, many of the seemingly pointless delays and setbacks we all experience contain lessons in persistence, humility, concentration, self-discipline, or some other quality whose importance is sometimes not obvious until years later. It is only in looking back on our lives from a distance we see how some frustrating or insurmountable roadblock was in fact what Princeton president James McCosh (1868–1888) liked to call a "fortuitous check," an event that kept us from taking a dangerous path or perhaps created an opportunity we had not imagined at the time.[123]

All we can know for sure is the individualized training program God has devised for each of us is not the discipline we would ever have picked for ourselves. Just as Moses would not have chosen to be led into Midian and kept there for forty years to be prepared to guide a nation—just as Abraham likely would not have wanted to wait until age seventy-five to birth the nation of Israel or Noah six hundred years to be ready for the flood—so each of us bristles against a regimen whose value presently eludes us.

Indeed, it is typically the highly intelligent or exceptionally talented person who has the greatest difficulty accepting this fact, which is why so many promising young people inexplicably self-destruct at the very beginning of their careers. The story of the rock singer who burns out accepting every gig or of the would-be entrepreneur who foolishly squanders his early profits on some hastily-conceived second act may be a cliché, but one that makes an important point about not trying to force a future not ready to happen.

What is most required of the most promising, MIT president Henry Smith Pritchett (1900–1907) tried to impress on the engineering students of his day, is to recognize how carefully God molds his earthly servants. It is patient, often halting and frustrating work that over the long run produces the result, not the meteoric shortcut.[124]

Augustus Hopkins Strong, president and professor of theology at the Rochester Theological Seminary from 1872 until 1912, liked to tell the story[125] of a student who once complained he was seeking Divine guidance in his work, but all his projects, no matter how well-intentioned, seemed to come up short. Doubting and discouraged, he feared his studies had come to nothing and desired to know what he should do.

This man's problem, Strong explained, was in looking for visible results. He forgot God's greatest gift is the knowledge that one is working with and for Christ: "While he has been looking outside for this thing or that, for this communication or that, he has been ignoring the fact that the one unspeakable gift of God is Christ himself."

In telling this story, Strong went on to confess that before he learned this lesson for himself, he typically worked in a "plodding, burdened, fearing, [and] distressful" way. "I had none of the joy that normally belongs to the Christian life," he admitted.

It was not until he pondered the Scriptural words "I am the vine; ye *are* the branches" (*John* 15:5) when Strong realized the early disciples were full of hope and power just because they knew Christ was in them. They lived by faith in the Son of God, regardless of immediately discernible results. In that moment, he learned the "secret of Christianity and it wrought a great transformation in my experience."

When a well-known Christian writer of our own time, the Catholic mystic Thomas Merton, learned a close friend had taken up a difficult challenge, he immediately advised his old acquaintance not to motivate himself with any hope of quick results. "When you are doing the sort of work you have taken on," Merton said, "you may have to face the fact that your work will be apparently worthless and even achieve no result at all, if not perhaps results opposite to what you expect. As you get used to this idea, you start to concentrate not on the results but on the value, the rightness...of the work itself." In this way, he concluded, "you can be more open to the power that will work through you without knowing it."[126]

Permanent Honor

True success—spiritual success—requires a trio of disciplines which keep us from succumbing to the soft atheism which is so prevalent in our time: forsaking excessive contingency planning, maintaining the courage to accept an arduous call, and seeing the wisdom in delays and setbacks. In return, Yale College president Noah Porter (1871–1886) annually assured his graduating seniors, the world "will, sooner or later, render to true men their permanent honor."[127]

Some years ago, I found my own way to make this same point in the context of a seminar on the connection between spiritual values and emotional health I often gave at churches, hospitals, and colleges around the country. Whether speaking to lay or professional audiences, I always began in the morning with a lecture on how so many psychological problems—anxiety, depression, fear, and guilt—stem from the subtle ways people compromise their religious values.

In the afternoon session, however, I had participants break up into small groups to discuss several questions related to the seminar topic. Finally, as the event wound down, I requested the attendees to perform one last task: "I'd like each of you to think of the person you admire most and then take turns explaining to the others in your group why you picked this individual. This person you look up to can be somebody living or from the past, someone well-known to the world or just a private association."

When everyone was finished, I would ask for one volunteer from each group to say out loud the name of the person he or she admired the most and the reasons why. Those identified varied widely: from Plato to Benjamin Franklin to Martin Luther King to Margaret Thatcher.

And, of course, many people mentioned parents, siblings, or teachers known only to themselves. But the underlying reasons for the admiration were far more consistent. Those held in highest esteem almost invariably had three qualities in common: they did not hedge their bets; they did not shy away from a challenge; and they certainly persevered regardless of initial setbacks.

Reflecting on what it is we respect in the people we most admire reveals much about how God wishes us to serve Him.

Reflection:

Trust in the Lord with all thine heart; and lean not unto thine own understanding. In all thy ways acknowledge him, and he shall direct thy paths.
—Proverbs 3:5–6

COPE SPIRITUALLY
WITH ADVERSITY

To mourn over an affliction [so] as to be thereby unfit for the discharge of present and future duties—what a complete perversion is it of all the real designs of earthly trial...! What a perversion of His design that, coming out from this nursery or gymnasium, weary and worn out with the discipline through which they have passed, they should lie down in listless inactivity!

*—Henry Darling, president of
Hamilton College (1881–1891)[128]*

In brief, as the mystics themselves often have said, sorrow—wisely encountered and freely borne—is one of the most precious privileges of the spiritual life. There is a certain lofty peace in triumphing over sorrow which brings us to a consciousness of what is divine in life in a way that mere joy, untroubled and un-won, can never make known to us. Perfect through suffering—that is the universal, the absolutely necessary law of the higher spiritual life.

—Braxton Craven, president of Duke University (1842–1863 and 1866–1882)[129]

One does not live for emergencies, but the emergency discloses what manner of life we have lived.

—Caroline Hazard, president of Wellesley College (1899–1910)[130]

"...ye shall have tribulation..."

From the founding of Harvard in 1636 up through the American Revolution, the Civil War, the westward expansion, and the First World War, the era of America's Christian college leadership was characterized by a series of social upheavals. But few presidents were as severely tested during this period as Atticus Greene Haygood.

Certainly, the circumstances of Haygood's upbringing gave little hint of the trials to come. Born 1839 in the village of Watkinsville, Georgia, he enjoyed a privileged childhood by the standards of his day.[131] His father was a prominent attorney, his mother a schoolteacher, and there were servants to help with household chores. In 1852, the family moved to Atlanta, where he attended Emory College. There Haygood courted and married a minister's daughter, studied theology, and, seven years later, began a promising career as a circuit preacher.

It was not until the Civil War in 1861 when young Haygood's seemingly untroubled life was thrown into turmoil, first during his service as a chaplain to the Confederacy and later as the pastor of Atlanta's Trinity Church. In 1863, he was harassed by paid agents from the North, who plundered Southern churches and then incited freedmen to riot with false rumors the local clergy were secretly plotting to re-enslave blacks. A year later, Haygood endured most of Atlanta being burned to the ground by General Sherman as well as the infamous slaughter and famine that followed. The very cemetery where his parents were buried was vandalized by Union forces.

Preaching a hopeful message in the wake of the South's devastating defeat was difficult enough for Haygood, but he also felt called upon to persuade surviving whites of the need for equal rights for all peoples. Appointed to the presidency of Emory College in 1876, he sermonized plantation owners on the morality of emancipation for their former slaves and wrote controversial pamphlets in favor of public education for everyone. In 1882, Haygood became a consultant to the reform-oriented John F. Slater Fund, which supported Booker T. Washington's Tuskegee Institute and subsidized the founding of other controversial schools in the old Confederacy.

While the Northern press praised Haygood for his forward-leaning views, at home he was viciously attacked as the "Nigger College President," falsely accused of fathering two illegitimate children by a black woman, and charged with slandering the South just to curry favor with wealthy Yankee philanthropists. From the end of the Civil War until 1890, when his election to the Southern Methodist episcopacy required a move to Los Angeles, Haygood's many good works were constantly called into question and his life was always in danger.

Yet for all these challenges, Haygood's infectious good humor and optimism never flagged. "The first ground I mention of my confidence in your success," he would tell Emory College's graduating seniors, is "there is not a genius among you. And what is better, there is not, unless I am greatly mistaken, among you a man who thinks himself a genius.... But many of you have what is better than genius—the spirit of hard-plodding, patient, all-conquering work. In this spirit is 'the promise and potency' of any achievement Providence calls you to attempt."[132]

Many observers attributed Haygood's persistent cheerfulness to the support of family, friends, and academic colleagues, for which he expressed unceasing gratitude. But whenever he was pressed to name the one thing most responsible for his buoyant outlook, he simply repeated the words Jesus famously spoke to his disciples in *John* 16:33: "In the world ye shall have tribulation...."

As pessimistic as this Biblical pronouncement strikes many a modern ear, Haygood knew from experience it really supplies a powerful emotional resilience. For once one accepts the fact that adversity is an inevitable part of life, the sufferings that come no longer leave the person feeling unfairly victimized or without the resources to cope. Steeled in advance for opposition and setbacks, one is no longer immobilized by them.

Forewarned is Forearmed

Consider another early college president who, before helping to found Antioch College, was the person we now credit with establishing the right of every citizen to receive a basic education. Appointed in 1837 as head of Massachusetts' newly-invented board of public instruction, Horace Mann (1853–1959) produced a series of reports for the teaching of reading, writing, and math that became the template for America's first public schools.

It's a lesser-known fact today, but Mann came close to making no historical contribution at all, for it was just a few years before his appointment when his beloved wife Charlotte died unexpectedly. Trying to press on with his law practice in the small Bay State town of Dedham, all the while serving as area representative to the state legislature and helping his heavily-indebted brother, Stephen, he became increasingly isolated, often sleeping in his office and skipping meals. His closest friends worried Mann had so lost any hope for the future he might even take his own life.

Fortunately for Mann, his reading of Scripture taught him to expect serious setbacks in life, but none so crippling that prayers for God's help would fail to point the way toward a new dawn. What this brighter future might look like, no one could know for certain, but intuitions would appear to guide the way.

In his own case, that guidance came as increasingly frequent thoughts of moving to nearby Boston. Mustering all his energy, Mann finally closed his law office in Dedham, resigned his seat in the legislature, sold what few assets he had, and traveled the sixteen miles to the city. There he found lodgings at a boarding house where, it turned out, his future wife Mary Peabody was also staying and soon received a job offer from the law firm of an old friend, Edward Loring. Requests also came in from old political acquaintances who wanted his help in drafting legislation.

Although still depressed by Charlotte's passing, Mann recovered enough by 1834 that friends encouraged him to run for the state Senate, which he did successfully. And so impressed were colleagues with his perseverance in the wake of personal tragedy that, even though a junior member, he was the majority's choice to be chamber president.

Three years later, Mann signed the bill creating America's first ever state board of education and, with its establishment, was urged to become its founding secretary. As hard as it was to accept the loss of his wife, Mann's understanding of the world as a place where even the most devoted believer's faith is likely to be tested led to a new life as, first, an education reformer, later a senator, and eventually a widely admired college president.[133]

Modern science has not yet gotten around to documenting the connection between the Christian's expectation of suffering and a superior capacity to cope with adversity; although, as with so many spiritual prescriptions, secular hints of the relationship can be found. Why, to take an obvious example, do police departments, schools, hospitals, and other public institutions hold periodic disaster drills, if not from the conviction that being forewarned is being forearmed?

Even more persuasive are the results of recent studies on what researchers call *psychological resilience*—the capacity of some people to bounce back from accidents, afflictions, or toxic environments overwhelming to most others. A relatively new field, it has nevertheless demonstrated that those who deal best with personal tragedies or serious economic setbacks are those who have learned to resist feeling unfairly victimized by adversity and who hold to the more spiritual proposition that bad things happen.

Such resilience is especially strong among those who were able to develop it early on, in response to a broken family, coping with a learning disability, or having an alcoholic parent. Social scientists "have found a surprising pattern among those whose early lives included tough times," says University of Virginia clinical psychologist Meg Jay. "Many draw strength from hardship and see their struggle against it as one of the keys to their later success. A wide range of studies…has shed light on how such people overcome life's adversities—and how we might all cultivate resilience as well."[134]

Writing on what he calls "Crucibles of Leadership" for the *Harvard Business Review*, the well-known management expert Warren G. Bennis summarized what he learned from in-depth conversations with more than forty of America's top executives over a three-year period. Like Jay, he too was "surprised to find that all of them—young and old" attributed their exceptional leadership abilities to the constructive outlook adopted in response to an earlier, often traumatic, life setback.[135]

"Everyone Disappoints You."

Years ago, I knew a minister who developed what seemed at the time to be an unnecessarily harsh approach to marriage counseling. At the end of each session with a newly engaged couple, he would stare into each partner's eyes and say, "Keep this in mind. Everyone disappoints you."

I can still remember the outrage I felt when I heard of this purported counseling technique. "How dare he say such a terrible thing on the eve of such a happy event!" I thought to myself. Yet, with time, I came to see the minister was only trying to fortify young couples with some very sage advice, the same advice an early American college president might have given, although perhaps with a little more sensitivity.

No matter how much one may love or appreciate his or her partner, the minister was telling engaged couples, that partner will eventually behave in a hurtful and disillusioning way. That is the human condition. And to the extent both are prepared for this to happen, the relationship is better fortified to absorb the blow.

I read recently of another minister who likes to share an instructive parable: It seems that two brothers were raised in a home with an abusive alcoholic father. The first brother grows up to be a violent drinker himself, while the other permanently swears off alcohol and is regarded by neighbors as a model parent. Yet when each brother was asked why he turned out the way he did, both replied the same. "Given who my father was, how could I not?"[136]

The minister's point was a simple but profound one. Everyone is destined to experience major setbacks, but not everyone responds to hurt in the same way. If there is one thing we can rely on, it is that misfortune is overcome better and faster when it is treated constructively.

The Great Illuminator

If the early college presidents' first principle for coping with adversity is to be forewarned of its occurrence, the second is very closely related to it—namely all tests, spiritually born, yield an unexpected blessing. The very fact that one learns endurance whenever his or her faith is tested, they would say is itself a priceless gift. In other words, quoting *James* 1:4, they would say, "... let patience have her perfect work, that ye may be perfect and entire, wanting nothing."

It was for this reason many presidents referred to suffering as "the Great Illuminator,"[137] by which they meant it enlarges and elevates the soul in unexpected ways. Joseph, sold into slavery by jealous older brothers, nevertheless became a better and wiser person for his imprisonment. Job was attacked by Satan yet, in clinging to his faith, eventually recovered all he lost and more. And, despite giving birth in a manger and later having to flee with her husband to Egypt, Mary gave birth to no less than the Son of God.

Of course, no president ever suggested adversity should be pursued for its own sake—life, it turns out, provides a more than adequate supply—but they did teach that every serious trial comes with a potential gift. Stanford University's first president, David Starr Jordan (1891–1913), was especially fond of telling his students about a children's book he read as a boy which listed in one column all the supposedly good personal qualities and in a second those generally considered bad. Among the good things were faith, hope, charity, piety, and integrity. Anger, selfishness, and trickery, on the other hand, were on the bad side of the ledger.

But among the positive things, Jordan said, the book put the term *adversity*, a positioning he at first thought must have been an editing or typesetting error. The word *adversity* did have an admittedly "pretty sound," he remembered thinking at the time, but surely its meaning "was the same as *bad luck*. How can bad luck be a good thing?"

It was not until years later, after he watched the course of many friends' lives, when Jordan realized the good or bad in adversity had less to do with the event itself, but what people made of it. Those who responded to setbacks with resentment or self-pity rarely seemed to gain anything from the experience. But those who took "hold of bad luck bravely," daily asking God for strength and direction, appeared to reap both wisdom and even a certain contentment from their hardships. "It is not in the luck, but in ourselves," he had to conclude, "that the badness is."[138]

An excellent contemporary illustration of president Jordan's observation comes from Pulitzer Prize-winning journalist Charles Duhigg.[139] Reacquainting himself with former Harvard Business School classmates at their fifteenth annual reunion, Duhigg noticed something that completely surprised him. Many of those who had been fortunate enough to go straight from graduate school to prestigious jobs at big venture-capital firms or New York investment houses conveyed "a lingering sense of professional disappointment. They talked about missed promotions, disaffected children, and billable hours in divorce court." One alum who earned $1.2 million a year confessed he "hated going to the office."

It was the also-rans of the class—the ones who failed to get the positions they wanted right after school—who "wound up with jobs that were both financially and emotionally rewarding." It seemed to Duhigg that these late bloomers had the good sense to treat their setbacks as learning opportunities, which proved far more valuable as time went on than anything that might have come from immediate success.

Up-and-coming jewelry and handbag designer Emily Moon certainly agrees with the importance of treating painful failures and setbacks as hidden opportunities. Failure has "taught me a lot," she says.[140] "God was refining a lot in my character and strengthening me. And I am so thankful for the failure that I've had to walk through, because it taught me so much more than any of our [company's] winning ever did."

One of the most interesting psychological discoveries of recent years is how closely the belief that loss can serve a higher purpose is linked to the time it takes to recover from that loss. In her work with those grieving the death of loved ones, for example, Professor Joan Berzoff of the Smith College School for Social Work found mourners who bring a positive narrative to the experience—focusing on the wonderful things the departed person taught them, for example, or seeing the passing as a sign of approval for contemplated changes—rebuild their lives relatively faster.[141]

Once more, the effect of such a positive outlook appears to be cumulative. In studies where she followed the lives of children for many years, Columbia University psychologist Lisa Miller has found young people raised to look for the hidden upside in life's adversities become adults with above-average cognitive skills.[142]

We need only reflect on our own enjoyment of novels and films about fictional characters coping with some unexpected disaster to realize how much we already intuit a constructive aspect to suffering. It seems perfectly believable to us at the end of the story that the characters who have optimistically braved the catastrophe are now better persons for their ordeal. We find it equally plausible that the pessimist who resentfully sees only "another raw deal" in his or her plight ultimately suffers the most.

No matter how materialistic modern society has become, something deep within all of us knows that happiness does not proceed on the line of least resistance, but of bucking up. Or as Oberlin College president Henry Churchill King (1902–1927) once wrote, "However hard our lot may seem, we certainly cannot improve it by...permitting ourselves the embittered spirit."[143]

"There are such things as spiritual presentiments."

The third principle for coping with adversity is to remember not all setbacks are obvious. The unexpected announcement of a neighbor's pending move may be more emotionally stressful than we thought possible. A seemingly small business loss may be the dimly-perceived harbinger of greater troubles to come. We may even have a medical problem whose symptoms seem minor yet unconsciously alert us to the hidden hazard. (A prominent physician at a Connecticut hospital near me once confided that a patient's feelings about his or her health are, by far, the most reliable predictor of underlying medical problems.)

That some of the worst setbacks in peoples' lives are camouflaged should, if we think about it, make perfect sense. If what we call reality is but an imperfect representation of the true universe beneath, then it follows that not every real loss will be clearly visible. There are times, in other words, we can find ourselves feeling depressed, put upon, or wary for no ostensible reason. We have not lost anyone dear to us. We have not received an obvious physical injury. There has been no major financial reversal. Indeed, we could even be at a place in our lives where others would say they envy our situation. Yet, for some inexplicable reason, we cannot agree.

If early twentieth century psychiatry retained any of the spiritual wisdom of the early college presidents, it was the recognition that adversity need not be apparent to be disabling; events which seem minor or even fleeting can profoundly disturb our well-being. However skeptical Sigmund Freud and his contemporaries may have been about religion, they at least recognized people can apprehend serious difficulties without being able to clearly articulate them. The great mistake of the first psychiatrists was not in positing the existence of unconscious problems, but in assuming they had to be the residue of some childhood trauma. Having confirmed the very spiritual idea that unseen forces can profoundly influence our emotions, the mental health professionals in Freud's time focused too narrowly on either dredging up long-repressed memories or on anesthetizing them chemically.

"There are such things as spiritual presentiments," president Braxton Craven (1842–1863 and 1866–1882) cautioned his Duke University students a half-century before modern psychiatry's supposed discovery of the unconscious mind. "A storm on the coast of Africa troubles the waves on the American shore. Rheumatic joints foretell the equinoctial better than the almanac. The forest moans before the storm-cloud rises above the horizon. So does the soul of man have admonition of coming evils or favors. Angels whisper to it, and the Holy Ghost prompts it. Bright lights, or thunderings or lightnings upon the horizon of the spirit, are never to be disregarded…. "[144]

I once had a psychology professor who told me about a study done with patients who were diagnosed as "paranoid." Wanting to be sure just how severely the subjects had deluded themselves into feeling persecuted, the research team went out to interview their relatives, friends, and business associates, double-checking the actual circumstances of the patients' lives. As it turned out, many who were clinically labeled as pathologically mistrustful really did, in fact, have something to be afraid of: an unscrupulous subordinate at work who was after their job, a supposed friend who was stealing money, or even a disturbed relative with malicious intent.

Over the years, many other studies have confirmed the human capacity to uncover hidden patterns and make them intuitively conscious. In a 2010 experiment, for example, Barnaby D. Dunn of the Medical Research Council Cognition and Brain Sciences Unit in Cambridge, England, designed a card game that was based on no obvious strategy, but instead forced participants to rely upon their hunches. Most players figured out how to get better over time and even win consistently, although they could not say exactly how they were doing it. They unconsciously discovered the right strategy, determined the appropriate moves, and instinctively signaled their conscious minds what to do.[145]

That intuition warns of dimly-perceived problems has been known for decades by marriage counselors. Many have had clients who admit to knowing their relationships were not going to work out *before* the wedding—they just couldn't give themselves a good enough reason to call it off. While many divorcees can point to any number of mistakes after the ceremony which culminated in a final split, in many cases the biggest mistake was ignoring the private doubts that surfaced before taking vows.

There is much to be said for taking seriously any gnawing reservation, no matter how trivial or irrational we imagine others would judge it to be. Certainly, no one ever made a problem worse by praying on a persistent hesitation or confiding it to a trusted companion. As often happens, the courage to address a seemingly "minor issue" morphs into a fuller awareness of a much greater difficulty that, once recognized, can be adequately dealt with.

Hidden Power

The fourth and final spiritual principle for coping with adversity is to remember what we learned in the previous chapter: serving God in the material world has the effect of quietly tilting future events in our favor. Faith may not be a magic potion eliminating every problem or making every dream come true, but it does have a subtle influence in those situations where other people's responses are also influenced by a spiritual outlook.

"A man who goes through society manifesting the life of God in his soul becomes a power by the words which he utters," DePauw University president Matthew Simpson (1839–1848) once put it. "[And] if I may so speak, by the very atmosphere that seems to surround him. God is with him, and other men seem to feel God may be with them also."[146] University of Wisconsin president John Bascom (1874–1887) referred to this power as "a strange energy, a conquering strength over things which before seemed stubborn, rock like, hardly subject even to fracture."[147]

In 2016, University of Connecticut anthropologist Richard Sosis and his colleagues conducted an experiment which so elegantly demonstrated this power it made national headlines. Altering one fifth of the images in a stack of portrait photos to show a cross around the person's neck or an ashen crucifix on the forehead, the researchers then gave the stack to several hundred subjects of varying religious and economic backgrounds, asking them to grade the faces in the pictures for trustworthiness. As part of the study, subjects were also asked to play a board game which required them to entrust money to another player they felt was honorable.

What most struck Sosis was all the photo faces displaying a cross evoked strong feelings of confidence, not only among Christian subjects, but among secular students and those of other faiths. As for the trust game, the sight of a cross hanging on another player doubled the money non-Christians were willing to invest in that person. And the Ash Wednesday cross increased the investment even more, by an added 38.5 percent.[148]

In the aftermath of such an experiment, we must ask ourselves the inevitable question: If the mere picture of a religious symbol can have a measurable effect on the outcome of a game, how much more on the real-world moral and spiritual choices of a true believer?

One of the most popular Hollywood movies ever made is director Frank Capra's *It's a Wonderful Life.* As many readers already know, it tells the story of a good man who thinks himself a failure for remaining stuck in a small town and never getting the chance to do bigger things in the outside world. Given the opportunity to see what life would be like had he never been born, he realizes not only how much he has helped so many others, but also how much they appreciate him.

It's a Wonderful Life is just a film, of course. But as the early college presidents knew, the effect it describes is very real. A "great principle finds illustration in the history of nearly every good man," president Stephen Olin (1834–1837) assured his Wesleyan University students. Let this person move into any community, and some of his new neighbors will automatically regard him with a combination of humor and skepticism. His motives will be suspect, his words misunderstood, his actions misrepresented, and his intentions condemned. But with time, even the doubters suspect "he is not so bad as he seemed; only odd and over-strict, but well-meaning. Still later…his good morals and even manners [come to be] appreciated. In the end, he is the peacemaker of his vicinity; and when men are on their death beds, they will have him pray with them, and leave him the guardian of their children."[149]

I know a generous and devoted Christian, who some years ago was convicted for federal income tax evasion. Ironically, it was his very generosity that helped get him into trouble. For in addition to failing to report certain reimbursed business expenses that were technically income, he had for many years given money to people who had either fallen on hard times or were involved in worthy social projects.

The government's problem with this later behavior was not the businessman's exceptional big-heartedness but the fact that he was writing off his gifts as tax-deductible contributions from his company, even though not every beneficiary qualified as federally-approved charity. And, while some might argue he was doing more good by giving money directly to the needy than to the government, the fact remains he was not rendering unto Caesar what was legally Caesar's.

But the most interesting part of the story was not the crime itself, but what happened toward the end of the court proceedings. Learning the judge would offer friends of the accused the opportunity to attest to his good character—in effect, to plead for a reduced sentence—many showed up at the appointed time with prepared speeches that turned out to be completely unnecessary. For when they arrived, the courtroom was already packed with 120 other people who had the same idea. It was, an old-time municipal guard said, the largest such gathering he ever saw.

For more than an hour and a half, the judge listened sympathetically to various pleas for mercy and then, before most of those who showed up had a chance to speak, unexpectedly banged her gavel. "If there were any way I could let you off, I would," she said, looking straight at the accused with a slight choke in her voice. "It's obvious, on balance, you are a credit to your community."

But, she went on, "even though you have admitted your crime and paid the treasury what you owe with interest, the law does require some period of incarceration, which I must now reluctantly impose." And so, he ended up with a twenty-eight-day sentence at a minimum-security facility where he became immediately involved in a Christian ministry that met four days a week and reached out to other inmates as well.

I always come back to this person's encounter with the law when I need to remind myself that the social power of faith is not a matter of being a saint or having an unblemished record. Even Christ's disciples included men who were once coarse, impulsive, excessively critical, self-absorbed, and greedy; and, while greatly changed in his service, never claimed moral perfection.

Fearing for his life, Peter himself immediately disguised his identity after Christ's arrest. Three times he denied he was in any way associated with Jesus and deliberately used foul language to prove it.

While it is always better to be good than to be bad, it is important to remember that God allows a lot of social credit for sincere efforts, however fitful. Daily falling short of perfection does not in of itself diminish one's spiritual aura. Only a complete denial of faith—or making perfection a precondition for further service—can accomplish that.

More difficult than giving a spiritual impression is being open-minded enough to recognize the help that our faith has, in fact, already elicited from others in our times of need. Like the George Bailey hero of *It's a Wonderful Life*—so desperate for money to pay off his savings and loan company losses he cannot see the eagerness of friends and neighbors to bail him out—we can be so fixated on our own conception of being Divinely rescued that we fail to spot the nearby lifeline.

An ancient parable, told and retold in many a sermon, tells the tale of a man who was shipwrecked on an island. Having lost his family and all his worldly possessions, he immediately begins to pray: "Dear God, please come and save me."

The man continues praying until one day a fisherman comes close to the island and calls out, "You poor man! Do not despair. I will take you home in my boat."

"Do not worry," the castaway yells back. "I have prayed to God, and I know he will not forsake me in this time of need. Go about your business."

Sometime later, a large freighter passes, and its captain, noticing the outcast's makeshift tent on the beach, draws closer to the island. Finally spotting a thin, malnourished man through his binoculars, the captain calls out, "I can see that you are starving, but do not worry. You can cruise back to civilization with us!"

But again, the shipwrecked man replies: "Do not worry. I have prayed to God, and I know he will not forsake me in this time of need. Go about your business."

Finally, a naval warship on a reconnaissance mission chances upon the island. Seeing a limp body lying nearly dead in the sand, the officer in command directs his vessel closer to shore and shouts, "You are clearly in trouble! I shall land and take you to safety!"

And for a third time the now barely-breathing castaway replies: "Do not worry. I have prayed to God, and I know he will not forsake me in this time of need. Go about your business."

The officer reluctantly complies; and soon after, the ship-wreck survivor, having suffered for so long without food, fresh water, and shelter, finally dies and goes to Heaven. There he meets God and asks in disbelief, "I kept faith, Lord, but you never came to help me. What did I do wrong?"

"I always answer my children's prayers," God replied. "And no less with you. Why did you not go with the fisherman, the freighter captain, or the naval commander I sent to save you?"

The message of this time-honored parable is clear: no matter how serious a dilemma we might find ourselves in, faith is an enduring power which predisposes others to intervene on our behalf. The trick is not to let our own preconceived notions of Divinely-engineered assistance blind us to the help already close by.

Reflection:

If any of you lack wisdom, let him ask of God,
that giveth to all men liberally, and upbraideth not;
and it shall be given him. But let him ask in faith,
nothing wavering. For he that wavereth is like a wave of
the sea driven with the wind and tossed. For let not that
man think that he shall receive any thing of the Lord.
A double minded man is unstable in all his ways.
—James *1:5–8*

DO NOT IMAGINE YOURSELF MORALLY EXEMPT

It is in these unseen struggles of the "inner man" that the world is to be conquered, and the flesh crucified, and the nature purified and disciplined, and made meet for Communion with God, and for the undefiled heritage which he has prepared for his children.

—Stephen Olin, president of Randolph-Macon College (1834–1837) and of Wesleyan University (1839–1841)[150]

The economies of human life are not, in the long-run, favorable to falsehood and pretension.

—Yale College president Noah Porter (1871–1886)[151]

> *Truth-speaking is not a recipe for making life easy but for making it worthwhile, [for] no one who has thoroughly tested the results of frank, accurate, reliable speech and action will want to go back into the vitiated air of lying....*
>
> —*William DeWitt Hyde, president of Bowdoin College (1885–1917)[152]*

What Harvard Wanted

Charles W. Eliot, the erudite and widely admired son of a wealthy Boston family, served as the president of Harvard University for a remarkably long forty years, from 1869 to 1909. But it took only a single moment for him to capture what all the early college presidents believed an essential feature of living spiritually in the material world.

It occurred the afternoon President Eliot was informed someone on the school baseball team had just pitched what everyone watching agreed was an exceptionally good curve ball. "I understand that a curve ball is thrown with a deliberate attempt to deceive," Eliot was said to have replied gravely. Then he added with a frown of disapproval, "Surely this is not the behavior we want to foster at Harvard."[153]

Baseball, of course, is just a game. And it is likely President Eliot was only pretending to be as concerned as he sounded to make a larger point. Yet his response showed the significance all the college presidents of his day attached to promoting high moral and ethical standards even—indeed, especially—in those situations where they are most easily compromised.

The real test of one's spiritual health, the presidents taught, is not in the refusal to kill or to rob or to commit some other offense so appalling that even the most secular authority would not hesitate to punish it. True character is the willingness to resist those temptations which occur on the margins of respectability or which are apparent only to oneself.

As Paul wrote to the church in Colossae, it is only when we strive to be morally accountable for all our actions, no matter how easily the failure to do so may be hidden from others, that we are in daily harmony with God's will. "And so whatever ye do, do *it* heartily, as to the Lord, and not unto men." (*Colossians* 3:23)

The enlightened soul, noted Eliot's contemporary, Princeton president James McCosh (1868–1888), grieves "far more over his lesser infirmities than others do over their greater" and discerns more clearly "the remaining evil in the heart and conduct." He or she knows the effort required to avoid telling even the most trivial white lie is neither time wasted nor being needlessly hard on oneself, but an investment in true self-advancement. Like the maid who was once asked how she knew she was really a committed Christian, the wise believer answers, "I now sweep under the mats."[154]

In our deference to the moral physics of the unseen, McCosh argued, we unleash powerful forces that, over time, cycle back to enrich our lives in countless ways—ways, while invisible to the eye, are nevertheless very real.[155] It might be on some future day, when we are in desperate need of a job, a position will be offered which, had we been content with a less honorable life, would not be available to us. Or perhaps at a time when we require advice about a pressing personal issue, we will conveniently bump into an old friend with just the answer we've been looking for.

What exactly our rewards will be is unknowable, since no human could ever predict the incredibly intricate train of circumstances connecting one's ethical behavior to its advantageous harvest. Indeed, to an outside observer the fortuitous developments resulting from our attempts to be a better person may never appear anything more than a series of "lucky coincidences"—although even the most cynical spectator would still have to admit our evident good fortune "could not have happened to a nicer person."

Conversely, the presidents argued, the habitual indulgence of even small character defects will have serious consequences for the broad trajectory of one's life. Moral failings have deep "structural" implication, Case Western Reserve president Charles F. Thwing (1890–1921) cautioned his own son, who had just entered college. A person may "think that there may be some weakness in one part of his whole being which shall not affect his whole being…that he can play fast and loose…without weakening his conscience or without impairing the truthfulness of his intellectual processes." But just as "the illness of one organ damages all organs," moral "weakness in one part results in weakness in, and for, every part."[156]

"His spirit will speak in the tones of his voice."

About as close as we can get today to illuminating the social physics of character involves the contemporary study of how a person's underlying purposes are made visible through gestures, voice inflection, and other aspects of his or her physical appearance. Regardless of any privately calculated advantage to telling a white lie, venting a resentment, or indulging some other dishonorable impulse, some truth of one's real intention always makes its way into the social environment, producing a chain reaction, first among the immediate observers and later their associates. Modern psychologists have adopted the phrase "body language" to describe this phenomenon although, as the presidents clearly knew, the idea goes back at least as far as *Proverbs* 16:30: "He shutteth his eyes to devise froward things: moving his lips he bringeth evil to pass."

"Every emotion and passion of man has an external expression, a visible impress upon the body and its motions," Duke president Braxton Craven (1842–1863; 1866–1882) explained body language to his own students, as he tried to give them a feel for the broader consequences of their spiritual behavior—or lack thereof. "This expression of the soul's character not only shows itself in the lines of the face, the proportions of the nose, the movement of the lips, and the movements of the body, but in the countenance, that indescribable illumination of face that shows the light and shadows of the invisible indwelling sun."[157] Covert intentions may not always be completely obvious, he added, but the reluctance to make eye contact, telltale arm or leg movements, or a defensive posture are enough to warn others of a moral compromise in the making.

It is a "too little pondered truth," Randolph-Macon College president John A. Kern (1897–1899) told his own students, that the real moral choice in life is not whether to be open with other people, but *how* to be open: to strive to be a person of integrity or to utter falsehoods whose untruthfulness is almost always, in some way, communicated. "Every man, whether he wills to do it or not, is continually pronouncing judgment, in the presence of other people, upon himself. His spirit will speak in the tones of his voice. His habit of thought and speech will write itself upon his face."[158]

Yale's Arthur Twining Hadley (1899–1921) liked to stress that the physical expressions of character are just as obvious at work as they are in one's personal life, especially for people in positions of authority. One cannot be a successful leader, he told his undergraduates, unless he strives to be a "revelation of God to his followers." If one is honest, regardless of how difficult that can sometimes be, "others are ready to accept his leadership and to regard his sayings and doings as revelations of the divine purpose." Every sacrifice of convenience, every refusal to smooth things over dishonestly becomes "in ways often unseen" an inspiration for co-workers to complete the task at hand.[159]

But once a would-be leader succumbs to the illusion he can successfully manipulate others, Hadley warned, he can "not disguise it," and the corrosive effects quickly multiply.[160] The willingness of employees to go the occasional extra mile, needed for any firm to create a good product, automatically evaporates whenever they suspect the boss lacks character.

If modern science has advanced on what the presidents taught about body language, it is the recent discovery that the more cleverly constructed an attempt to deceive, the more likely it is to be sensed. This is because well-disguised lies are harder to decipher and have the ironical effect of challenging the person on the receiving end to figure out what is happening. Even what the deceiver believes to be a minor or benevolent white lie—something said to spare a friend's feelings about a bad haircut or mismatched wardrobe—is experienced by others as a psychological red alert, an alert to immediately understand the message behind the message.

It is precisely the difficulty of lying successfully which has led airlines around the world to train their crews in how to be more direct and assertive. These companies have learned from experience that deliberately downplaying a mechanical issue on the ground or the severity of an inflight problem only causes the passenger to worry far more than if he or she heard the truth. Health-care providers have also become aware of how soft-pedaling a medical diagnosis will alarm patients much more than a straightforward presentation of the facts.[161]

"The connection does not immediately appear."

The presidents understood that most people are, unfortunately, either sufficiently polite—or insufficiently capable of proving what they only sense—to openly accuse someone else of exhibiting bad character. The result is that the would-be manipulator is lulled into thinking one's self uniquely talented when it comes to skirting moral boundaries. He or she may even imagine the power to mislead others whenever it seems convenient.

Ironically, the people most vulnerable to this illusion are often those most respected for their service to the community—doctors, teachers, government officials, and even minis-ters. Their delusion that they can camouflage character lapses is encouraged, not only by the reluctance of average people to criticize someone with a high or revered social status, but also by their own belief that hard work and sacrifice has entitled them to a certain moral leeway. "I am giving so much to others," the accomplished humanitarian will say to himself. "I'm so busy. So why shouldn't I cut myself some slack on this or that small thing? I'm only doing it for a good reason and I'm clever enough to pull it off, so what's the point of being so hard on myself? Anyway, no one else will notice."

Unfortunately, society's tendency to silently tolerate minor ethical transgressions persuades all of us that we have a greater margin for moral compromise than we really do. "Virtues, when traced in all their relations, are found to form important links in the chain of general happiness," Princeton University president Samuel Stanhope Smith (1795–1812) annually cautioned the seniors in his moral philosophy class. But for most, he added sadly, "the connection does not immediately appear."[162]

More than a century later, Stanford University's founding president David Starr Jordan (1891–1913) would give the same warning to his own students. Much of human misery, he told them, stems from the common illusion that the world grants us a wider latitude than enjoyed by others, that somehow or another God will "make an exception in our favor. We are prone to think that nature will ease up somehow in our own case.... The laws of right were intended for someone else. [That we enjoy] some kind of special indulgence...."[163]

Forestalling Disaster

One of the most important questions posed by the early college presidents was whether it is possible to learn that one is not morally exempt without having to experience some reformatory calamity. Was there, in other words, some way to learn the advantages of improved character without having to be severely punished for remaining willfully blind?

Many presidents were encouraged to think so by the insights of Ignatius of Loyola, a sixteenth century Spanish monk whose book of *Spiritual Exercises* was written to help readers cultivate a more vivid appreciation for the moral physics beneath everyday appearances. Although he was a Catholic—indeed, the founder of an order that worked to counteract the Protestant Reformation—his belief in the possibility of detecting enough of the underlying spiritual reality to be changed by it captured the imaginations of Christians throughout Europe.

Even in England, where authorities attempted to ban his *Spiritual Exercises* in the wake of growing conflict with Spain, smuggled copies of the book influenced such popular writers as John Donne, George Herbert, and Richard Crashaw. So much so that when the Puritans and other persecuted religious minorities set sail for the New World, Ignatius's ideas went with them, eventually to surface in the lectures and writings of early America's college presidents.

What especially influenced the presidents' thinking was Ignatius's description of the incident that turned his own life around. The year was 1521, and he was still a young man serving the Spanish crown as a military commander. Eventually suffering a near-fatal wound in a battle against French forces near the town of Pamplona, Ignatius was compelled to retreat to his family's castle to recuperate.

Even before joining the army, Ignatius had a well-deserved reputation for being contentious and spiteful. One time, during a disagreement between the Loyolas and another prominent family, he led a few relatives in a violent nighttime ambush of some clerics who were members of the other clan. This outrageously thuggish tactic was so offensive to local authorities that he was forced to flee town and hide out until the charges against him were finally dropped, apparently on a technicality.

Now condemned to a painfully long and boring convalescence from his battlefield wounds, the thirty-year-old Ignatius found himself yearning for any distraction he could find. When he asked his caretakers for a few romantic adventure novels to help him pass the time, it turned out the only two books immediately available were an account of the life of Jesus and a history of the great saints. Desperate for any diversion, he started reading, only to find himself alternating between excerpts from the religious manuscripts he had no interest in and fantasies of revenge against the French commanders who had humiliated him in battle.

It was while he was lying in bed alone, increasingly aware of how his mood changed as he switched between these two very different distractions, when Ignatius noticed something that changed his life—and more than a century later, the thinking of American college presidents: His daydreams of conquest, even when he imagined himself rewarded by the favor of a beautiful noblewoman, left him feeling dejected and unsatisfied. Yet, whenever he reflected on what he reluctantly read about the work of the saints and the ministry of Christ, he was surprisingly at peace with himself.

The more Ignatius attended to these two contrasting states, the more he could see the seeming excitement generated by fantasies of revenge was really the onset of a self-inflicted depression, while the spiritual accounts he was so reluctant to read were, in fact, a source of satisfaction. By attending to his own experience in a more systematic way than he ever did before, he became conscious of a stronger connection between religious values and worldly happiness than he ever imagined possible.

"Progress gives force as force makes progress."

To America's early college presidents, the lesson of Ignatius's self-experiment was both simple and obvious: the way to become a better person was simply to try it. Pick any character flaw, try one's best not to resort to it for a while, and then just notice how life seems to miraculously change for the better.

"The great power of the truth in the world is the individual life—the inner life of the individual as [revealed by] righteous personal living among men," Yale University president Timothy Dwight V (1886–1899) would sermonize in the school's chapel. "Your greatest power," he told the undergraduates, "lies in your ceasing…to be what you were as an unconverted man, and in being the opposite."[164]

Was this not what the apostle Paul was getting at when he told the Ephesians to let "all bitterness and wrath and anger and clamor and railing be put away from you, with all malice?"

Dwight suggested. Was he not inviting them to see for themselves how the world changes when a person tests the habit of speaking the truth to his or her neighbors...of forsaking covetousness and resentment...of blocking any impulse to steal...or of refusing to indulge any other dishonorable impulse?

We miss the point when we think of character development as the mere bucking up to reluctantly do what a stern God expects of us and not as the means for the total transformation of life, Dwight would conclude. To "put off the old man" and "put on the new man" is to run a grand self-experiment, one with the potential to permanently change the way we experience and, therefore want to treat, the world.

Be therefore "kind, tender hearted, forgiving each other," Dwight advised. "If you are a child, obey your parents, and honor them. If you are a father, see that you do not provoke your children. Whatever your condition, walk in that condition worthily of the calling wherewith you were called.... This was the work which [Paul] gave these early Christians to do; and as they did it...the Church grew in numbers and in power."[165]

Like all the other early college presidents, Dwight knew full well no one could ever perform such a self-experiment perfectly—no human could. But perfection is not the goal, only a sufficient awareness of the renovating effect to further fortify one's moral courage. The metaphor favored by nineteenth-century presidents was the great technological achievement of their time, the railroad engine. Character, they said, is like a locomotive. It requires time and patience to get going, but once under way, it makes its own steam. "Progress gives force as force makes progress," as they put it.[166]

The Mansion of Happiness

It is hard to exaggerate the influence of the presidents' moral therapy or the enthusiasm with which it was accepted. When Benjamin Franklin's memoirs were published in 1791, revealing his own youthful experiment with self-imposed humility, few had any reason to doubt its effect. Indeed, Franklin's account of how he subdued his arrogant thoughts, making him both a better and happier person (see Chapter 8), quickly became required reading for every American school child and remained so for more than a century.

In 1843, the Boston firm of W. and S. B. Ives brought to market a colorful board game that for nearly five decades was symbolic of just how enthusiastically the American public embraced the presidents' moral psychotherapy. Called *The Mansion of Happiness,* it had players race along a sixty-six space track to get to the garden of a large estate in the center of the board, where men and women were pictured joyfully playing music and dancing. Directions on virtue spaces, such as "temperance," "honesty," and "generosity," moved contestants closer to this goal, while landing on vice spaces with names like "idleness," "ingratitude," and "immodesty" required them to retreat. The game was appropriately played with a small top inscribed with numbers—not dice, which in those days would have been associated with illegal gambling.

In its initial run, *The Mansion of Happiness* sold just three-to-four thousand copies, mostly through bookstores and dry goods shops. But within a few years, the game became so popular other companies, including Parker Brothers, released their own versions, all based on the premise of a connection between self-conscious moral restraint and the good life. *Mansion* was kept in production for more than half a century and successfully reissued in 1894 when Parker Brothers finally obtained the rights from Ives.

Enduring Wisdom

So evident were the psychological benefits of self-imposed character improvement that, even after the era of the Christian college presidents, a succession of popular self-help movements continued to promote it. Founded in 1921 by a Lutheran pastor named Frank Buchman, the *First Century Christian Fellowship*—nicknamed the *Oxford Group* when reporters mistakenly connected it to England's famous university—attracted tens of thousands of adherents with the simple premise that most unhappiness could be cured through moral self-experimentation. Buchman urged his followers to be more honest in all their affairs, to forsake judging themselves or others, to confess moral and ethical lapses in meetings with other members, to make amends for past wrongdoings, and to seek God's guidance through prayer, meditation, and conversation with other Christians.

According to press accounts of the day, the Oxford Group had no official membership list, no dues, no paid leaders, and no specific denominational affiliation, or regular meetings, just a willingness to meet regularly in small local groups for mutual encouragement. Wealthier members traveled the world at their own expense, trying to stimulate interest in the movement; and Buchman himself attended the 1936 Berlin Olympics in a daring, if naïve, attempt to rehabilitate Nazis. Publications from the *New York World-Telegram* newspaper to *Good Housekeeping* magazine continued to provide favorable coverage until the 1940s when America's entry into the Second World War brought the public's interest in self-help movements to a temporary close.

Interest in deliberate character improvement as a form of psychotherapy was again revived in the mid-1960s, this time by a disparate coalition of mental health professionals. Disillusioned by how little they were able to accomplish with psychoanalysis, behaviorism, drugs, and other materialistic therapies, many psychologists, psychiatrists, and social workers began having patients meet in small groups, where they could experiment with being more honest, tolerant, and intuitive, then hopefully carry the lessons they learned into their everyday lives.

For almost a decade, what came to be known as the "human potential movement" was not just a clinical technique, but a cultural phenomenon. Spiritually themed self-help books topped the bestseller lists, and Americans who could afford it flocked to weekend retreats like California's Esalen Institute for the opportunity to pre-test the experience of being more open amongst strangers whom they would never have to see again. Despite the frequent confusion of moral self-experimentation with the more sensational aspects of the '60s counter-culture—as well as a general ignorance of its religious origins—some form of systematic character development was subsequently adopted by almost every school of psychotherapy.

Coming down to today, we need look no further for a vibrant expression of the early college presidents' moral prescription than the success of Alcoholics Anonymous and other substance abuse programs, which have helped tens of millions of addicts get sober by encouraging them to take a moral inventory of their lives and behave better going forward. Indeed, the demand for space to accommodate AA meetings, as well as similar gatherings for the treatment of drug abuse, compulsive gambling, and overeating, is so great that providing it has become the most prevalent form of community outreach by America's Christian churches.

The good news for non-addicts is that the benefits of moral self-experimentation do not require any kind of formal meetings or professional guidance, simply the willingness to *act as if* one believed in the value of cultivating some moral or ethical trait until, lo and behold, the value becomes obvious. The procedure is very simple, says psychologist Rick Hanson, senior fellow at the University of California, Berkeley's Greater Good Science Center. It boils down to taking the risk to be a better person, making the effort a little longer than feels comfortable, and then paying attention to how one's life has changed as a result.[167] The only thing the early college presidents would add to this formula is remembering to give thanks to God for the enlarged vision of life it produces.

Believing that many people have learned to do something like this on their own, especially with respect to overcoming resentment, Tim Herrera, who edits the "Smarter Living" column in the *New York Times*, recently posed a question on his Twitter account: Had anyone "ever given up on a grudge" and, if so, how did it make them feel.

As one might expect from a Twitter group, Herrera later reported, "The responses were delightfully all over the place." But his favorite was the most introspective: "I felt very, very mature. I admitted that my feelings were valid for the situation at the time but allowed myself to reshape my thinking/attitude based on my personal growth experiences since then." It sounds like a cliché, the Twitter follower admitted, but "physically, I felt lighter."[168]

Of course, the modern cynic would counter that practicing positive character traits can indeed make a person feel good about oneself, but such naïve optimism inevitably backfires as one comes up against the real world's harsher realities, especially at work. Yet, to the extent intentional character development has been studied scientifically, the results suggest a very different conclusion. Just as in the college presidents' time, people who more rigorously practice traditional religious values do, in fact, become more successful than those who do not.

In 2015, scholars from the United States and Europe looked at the career trajectories of executives who placed a premium on having good values in their business dealings. In addition to being seen by colleagues as natural leaders, the "nicer" managers performed significantly better in performance reviews by their bosses.[169]

People with strong values even seem to be healthier than average. Not only do they have lower blood pressure, fewer instances of back pain, better weight control, and more desirable blood sugar levels, but they are also more emotionally resilient to unexpected setbacks.[170]

The medical benefits of cultivating good character is especially clear when it comes to forgiveness. In 2007, Virginia Commonwealth University researcher Everett Worthington and his colleagues published a literature review[171] which listed all the scientifically documented consequences of overcoming the desire for revenge. It turns out that people who work at forgiving others have a reduced risk of both physical and emotional illness, including substance abuse.

Other studies have found that hostility raises the risk of inflammation and chronic illness as one grows older and may, in addition, seriously stress both the immune and cardiovascular systems. On the other hand, says Dr. Frederic Luskin, Senior Consultant in Health Promotion at Stanford University, "full forgiveness can more or less reverse these negative repercussions of holding into anger and grudges."[172]

The Mysterious Link

Today's America has come a long way from the time when even little children playing board games understood that happiness comes from treating moral dilemmas, not as irritating obstacles to be expediently dispatched, but as opportunities to engage reality at its deepest level. Unfortunately, even many nominally religious people now seem to believe bending traditional values—"being smart about life"—has some advantage in the larger world beyond home and church. Despite the wisdom of the world's greatest novels, its most inspirational biographies, and of course Scripture, our present culture largely confines its moral ambition to those therapeutic settings where people have been most damaged by the lack of it.

Perhaps the person who best describes the modern American dilemma is not an American at all but Aleksandr Solzhenitsyn, the late Russian novelist, Christian apologist, and heroic critic of the old Soviet Union. Choosing the 1978 Harvard Commencement to make his first public statement in the United States after being deported by the Kremlin, Solzhenitsyn surprised the assembly by saying nothing of his experience with communist totalitarianism. Instead, he chastised the deluded smugness of Western materialism and the degree to which American culture had forsaken the spiritual wisdom of its past.

What America desperately needs, he believed, is a widespread and revolutionary return to "inward development," which, if it happened, would be a social advance "comparable to the transition from the Middle Ages to the Renaissance." Not a bloody or even physical revolution, but a "moral revolution," a "change from spiritual dispersal to spiritual concentration."[173]

The good news is that no one person's ability to benefit from such a transformation is limited by the larger society's opinion on the subject. All that is required is the willingness to self-experiment long enough for experience to become the most trusted teacher. In the words of Hamilton College president Henry Davis (1817–1833), "the courses which have conducted the virtuous to honor and felicity will, if faithfully pursued, conduct you to them also."[174] Or as the presidents so often said, quoting the apostle Paul: "Prove all things; hold fast that which is good." (*1 Thessalonians* 5:21)

The government of God is over all his works, Paul was saying. It links moral law to world outcomes in ways that may be complex and invisible, but hardly unreliable. By a means eternally mysterious, character is bound to destiny.

Reflection:

But seek ye first the kingdom of God, and his righteousness;
and all these things shall be added unto you.
—Matthew 6:33

SEEK NO SUBSTITUTE FOR AMENDS

[You] are your brother's keepers; and it matters nothing what may be your circumstances, you can never be absolved from the obligation to respect this principle…. It is of little consequence what the men of another spirit and other principles think or say about this matter. There is a witness in every man's conscience to the propriety and the importance of this rule; and that witness you never can…reason down or bribe to silence.

—Samuel W. Fisher, president of Hamilton College (1858–1866)[175]

Many indeed are the expedients devised to quiet conscience…but, at best, they are mere expedients, doing no credit to the hearts or heads of those who

*use them. The only honorable course is candidly to
confess your error, and to express your regret.*

—*John Maclean Jr., president of
Princeton College (1854–1868)[176]*

*Be not deceived, therefore, by imagining that
conscience, or moral sense, is the creation of
education—a mere adventitious acquisition. God
has not rested the virtue and happiness of his rational
creatures on so uncertain a foundation. Conscience
is as much an original power of our nature as the
[intellect].... You carry in yourselves the incitement,
the rule, and the reward. By admitting that the
moral sense springs up from the original frame of
your nature, you cannot avoid the obligation of doing
right, nor the censure and misery of doing wrong.*

—*Jonathan Maxcy, president of
Brown University (1792–1802)[177]*

The Universal Delusion

Of all the materialistic delusions, perhaps the most common is the idea that the guilt we feel over physically or emotionally harming another person can be assuaged in some way other than making amends directly to that person—or, if that is not possible, to God. The *Old Testament* tells us Cain tried lying his way out of taking responsibility for his brother's murder and it has been the human temptation ever since to imagine pangs of conscience can somehow be repressed, drugged senseless, bought off, negotiated down, left in the past, or otherwise tamed.

From the founding of America's first colleges, their presidents were acutely aware of the problem. The first impulse of all sinners, wrote Yale's Timothy Dwight IV shortly after the War for Independence, is "to quiet their consciences, either by mixing with companions whose conversation and pursuits may enable them to forget their alarms…or [by persuading] themselves that the doctrines and denunciations of the Scriptures are to be understood with many qualifications and softenings [so] that their case is therefore not so bad as they had been accustomed to suppose it."[178]

For all their love of progress, which they believed to be a Divine blessing on a faithful citizenry, the early college presidents knew it misled many into thinking they could run their lives independent of Scriptural wisdom. In the case of guilt, ever cheaper and faster modes of transportation made life more convenient, but it also created the illusion of being able to evade remorse by fleeing the scene of a moral crime. It was not a coincidence, they believed, that the invention of steamships and railroads in the early 1800s gave rise to popular novels in which rebellious children, escaped criminals, fallen women, and military deserters found a "second chance" out West.

By the dawn of the twentieth century, the presidents looked with even greater concern on the coming of the automobile and commercial aviation, both of which further enhanced the illusion guilt can be treated geographically. "Moral sufferings may be postponed in more ways and longer than other emotional issues," wrote University of Wisconsin president John Bascom (1874–1887) in his book *The Science of Mind*, seemingly cured by changed circumstances.[179] But the guilt "still surges," he warned, "not loud, but deep."[180]

And if the presidents recognized the spiritual challenge posed by advances in transportation, they were also ambivalent about America's continually rising standard of living. Ever-increasing prosperity, which had blessed the North American continent since colonial times, inspired its people to be commendably generous, but it also led many to imagine they could palliate a sense of regret in one area of their lives by doing something philanthropic in a completely different venue.

"You have seen," president Samuel Johnson (1754–1763) warned his Columbia College students in the years leading up to American independence, "what a blessed thing it is to give rather than to receive. But let the giver remember [that] there is a danger of losing that blessedness, if he is not influenced by right considerations.... Take care to be meek and humble, to avoid priding [yourselves] in them or thinking to merit by them, much less to atone for any instances of known wickedness."[181]

A century later, during one of his Sunday sermons in the Princeton College chapel, president James McCosh (1868–1888) returned to Johnson's point, counselling undergraduates that any attempt to buy off guilt with a charitable act inevitably fails. "Cease, I beseech you, from these efforts to construct a righteousness of your own," he told them. "[The] idol you set up is like the image seen by Nebuchadnezzar: the toes being part of iron and part of clay, which did not cleave one to another, and the whole was 'broken to pieces together, and became like the chaff of the summer threshing-floors, and no place was found for them.'"[182]

McCosh could already see how the great wealth produced by the Industrial Revolution was strengthening a misguided tendency to equate philanthropy with atonement. Not only were many prominent investors and businessmen attempting to rehabilitate their reputations for questionable dealings by financing libraries, hospitals, bridges, and other public works, but skyrocketing incomes in general made it easier for ordinary church-going Christians to entertain the possibility of buying absolution.

What the public did not see was how often some well-known industrialist would turn to his local minister to ask why the peace-of-mind he assumed would follow a generous charitable contribution failed to materialize. For no philanthropic gesture, regardless how much the newspapers might praise it as a model of civic virtue, can release a guilty conscience from its precipitating transgression.

"Innate in the Heart of Man"

The modern computer term *hardwired* did not exist in 1901, but Stanford University's David Starr Jordan (1891–1913) invented a close spiritual analog when he described conscience as a mechanism implanted by God in the human mind to automatically register His displeasure with morally injurious acts. "The force that punishes sin," he wrote, "is innate in the heart of man."[183]

Like all the other Christian college presidents, Jordan knew guilt grows out of the very constitution of one's nature and its relation to eternal law. Our inner morality does not suffer us to enjoy the esteem of others when we have fallen below a certain standard; neither can the pangs of conscience be put off, cheated, or bribed away. The mechanics of regret are deep inside us, a function of the soul. There is a witness in every mind, he said, that can never be completely reasoned away or bribed into silence. We are our brothers' keepers; and no matter what our circumstances, we are never absolved from respecting this principle.

Fashionable opinion about the psychology of guilt may vary with the times, Jordan taught his students, but fashionable opinion is irrelevant to the reality of what a serious moral or ethical violation causes one to feel. The majority in every age will judge themselves harshly for betraying another soul, regardless of what social philosophy happens to be in vogue. There is a part of every thief, of every thoughtless gossiper, and of every emotional abuser which desires to make amends for the damage he or she has done.

Were Jordan alive today, he would likely argue even a so-called *sociopath*—that rare individual who seems capable of acting without remorse—at least knows enough to accurately predict what others will think and feel when he crosses certain lines. In other words, his internal signaling system, no matter how damaged or dysfunctional, still gives testimony to the reality of an inbred moral sense.

Every mental health professional in our own time has at least one story like the case of an Air Force sergeant from Washington, DC, whose seemingly intractable problems were suddenly and remarkably improved by his decision to make amends for a long-simmering guilt.[184] The unhappy soldier started therapy with a local psychologist by voicing complaints about endless arguments with his wife, his son's emotional difficulties, and his own inability to stop philandering.

For months, the therapist tried to help the sergeant, but nothing seemed to work. Then one day, without any prompting, the sergeant decided to begin visiting his parents, who lived in nearby Baltimore. He talked with each of them separately, deliberately forsaking old battles, and confessing many things he had long kept secret.

The result of the sergeant's brave, if unsolicited, attempts to atone for his past was a spontaneous reversal in many of the complaints he originally brought into therapy. As it turned out, the sergeant's parents were not at all uncomfortable with his confessions, but he was noticeably more cheerful and animated. His marriage improved, and soon, he was ready to terminate therapy.

How often have any of us—perhaps because of too much wine at dinner or just the lateness of the hour—admitted a long-ago misdeed to a person we once harmed, only to feel an unexpected jolt of energy, as if the whole of life was temporarily elevated to a higher plane? The crime we acknowledged was likely a minor one and easily forgivable at such a late date, else the confession would not so easily have passed our lips. But if such a small admission can have such a dramatic emotional effect, what greater relief do we deny ourselves by the reluctance to address more serious transgressions?

The Great Blessing

Our wish that guilt might somehow be assuaged without directly addressing the person harmed is not hard to understand. The act of making amends is an intrinsically humbling one, for it means admitting to the person harmed we at least sensed we were doing wrong at the time we did it—and did it anyway. It means facing up to the fact we were not nearly as decent a person as we pretended to be.

Many of the early college presidents were especially fond of the section in Dante's classic, *The Divine Comedy*, where the author illustrates the universal reluctance to acknowledge guilt— and the depth of suffering people willingly endure just to skirt a confession of wrongdoing. It is the point in the poem where the narrator has been led down to the second circle of Hell. There he meets the beautiful Francesca and her lover Paolo, both of whom have been condemned to be buffeted in the windiest part of the underworld until they can finally admit responsibility for the adultery they committed in life.

The character of Francesca was based on a real person from Dante's time, an aristocrat named Francesca da Rimini. She was pressured by her family to marry a much older man and ended up having an affair with his younger brother Paolo, who was also married. The relationship went on for more than a decade when Francesca's husband finally surprised the couple in bed and killed them both.

When he first meets the fictionalized Francesca, the poem's narrator has some sympathy for her plight. Her marriage was politically arranged and her husband was both unattractive and abusive. But when the narrator asks why she cannot now confess her infidelity, it becomes clear her pride is still standing in the way. Eulogizing love as if it were a drug with irresistible hypnotic powers, Francesca stubbornly insists her murder and banishment to the second circle of Hell were due to forces beyond her control. At the end of the conversation, the reader is left with the impression of an intelligent woman who nevertheless cannot bring herself to make the confession that would free her from the howling winds.

Coming much closer to our own time, the late O. Hobart Mowrer, a former president of the American Psychological Association, never ceased to be amazed at how much pain guilt-ridden patients would endure to avoid confessing their misdeeds. Some would even be willing to undergo treatments like electroshock therapy in the hope its debilitating consequences would preclude the need to come to terms with the harm they caused.

Failing attempts to literally torture away their guilt, many would contrive a pseudo-confession with which they could pat themselves on the back for being "open and honest" without making an actual apology. One patient, a thirty-eight-year-old man who came into therapy for a variety of marital problems, finally decided to provide his wife the details of a series of affairs he was involved in over the years—but stopped short of expressing regret or asking her forgiveness. He hoped it would be enough to bring as much of his secret life as he could remember out into the open.

In the end, Mowrer observed, even a pseudo-confession does little to relieve a guilty conscience. In the case of the man who described his extramarital encounters to his wife, there was a temporary sense of relief because she reacted so well. But within weeks he felt "the weight of the world on his small shoulders again."[185] As much as the patient tried to just "accept himself" for what he did, he eventually asked to be committed to a psychiatric hospital.

As Mowrer put it, a person who gets to the point of acknowledging his guilt has made real progress, but he is not at liberty to just stop: "All our efforts to reassure and accept him will avail nothing. He will continue to hate himself and to suffer the inevitable consequences of self-hatred" until he has actually made amends.[186]

The Great Consolation

One of the great consolations of the Christian faith is the realization we are all sinners, each of us capable of betraying our fellow creatures, albeit in diverse ways. This knowledge by no means absolves us from responsibility for our misdeeds; but it does make the challenge of translating our wrongs into rights a far less humiliating task. Our moral failure has not branded us "inhuman," only "too human."

Furthermore, as the early college presidents were quick to assure their students, God has not left us in the dark about what needs to be done. Scripture tells us in cases where a misdeed involves something of monetary value—failing to guard a possession entrusted to our care, finding and keeping a neighbor's lost possession, or just plain theft—the remedy is mercifully straightforward: "…he shall restore…the thing which he hath deceitfully gotten, or that which was delivered him to keep, or the lost thing which he found, or all that about which he hath sworn falsely." (*Leviticus* 6:4–5) The *Old Testament* even suggests an appropriate surcharge to compensate the rightful owner for his or her inconvenience: a fifth of the value of the principal.

Restitution becomes admittedly more complex when money is not the issue or at least is not the only issue. And it becomes subtler still when the amends consist of little more than an apology, but the context in which it could be offered is problematic. Consider the woman who years ago spread a vicious rumor which led to the firing of a rival at work: Can she risk admitting the truth to the injured party while she is still employed at the same firm?

What if the person once harmed lives far away? Should the apology be offered in person? By phone? Or perhaps in a letter? Here too we are saved by a faith which recognizes, while no one is wise enough to calculate a perfect restitution, confiding in another believer—a trusted friend, spouse, teacher, pastoral counselor, or minister—sufficiently elevates our spiritual intelligence to solve the problem.

When today's Christian hears the word *fellowship*, he or she is most likely to recall those passages in Scripture where early believers joyously feasted together and prayed. "And they, continuing daily with one accord in the temple, and breaking bread from house to house, did eat their meat with gladness and singleness of heart...." (*Acts* 2:46) But the Biblical word for fellowship—*koinonia*—also prescribed a reliance on others for creative solutions to complicated problems: "And let us consider one another to provoke unto love and to good works: Not forsaking the assembling of ourselves together, as the manner of some *is*; but exhorting *one another*: and so much the more, as ye see the day approaching." (*Hebrews* 10:24–25)

I once met a woman who for years felt guilty because of an abortion in her early twenties. In the back of her mind, she always wanted to make amends to her unborn child, an idea she repeatedly discounted as "too far out" until a local minister she consulted persuaded her not to be so dismissive of the intuition. Working together, they soon came up with the idea of a belated funeral service, which the minister was willing to perform. Having finally given her child the proper burial she felt she owed it, the crippling guilt she suffered for so long began to dissipate.

British writer Mark Greene tells the story[187] of a man who discovered the right amends to make by listening to the very person he offended. The man was in the Far East on business and, as is the custom when closing a deal in that part of the world, went out for drinks with his customers at a bar featuring attractive hostesses. Toward the end of the evening, after more than one-too-many drinks, the man uncharacteristically propositioned one of the girls, whose protest at being thought "that kind of woman" instantly sobered him.

Now feeling terribly guilty about how thoughtlessly crude he had been, the man was relieved when the hostess said she was having some personal problems and needed some advice. As it turned out, he stayed up with her until three in the morning just talking and letting her share all her sadness about just recently breaking up with a boyfriend.

Although not nearly as well-known as it should be, there is one organization which for over seventy-five years has been offering spiritual fellowship to workers whose burdens of guilt have led to chronic alcoholism, drug abuse, and other self-destructive behaviors. It began in the late 1930s, when a loose confederation of executives formed the Occupational Alcohol Program (OAP) to reach out to problem drinkers at every corporate level.

The group quickly discovered the most effective counselors were not licensed mental health professionals but former drunks who became sober through Alcoholics Anonymous—a spiritual self-help program which emphasizes making amends to the people one has seriously harmed. Drawing on their own experience with guilt, these recovered addicts were able to guide still active drinkers in atoning for their own misdeeds, thereby removing much of the incentive to get high.

By 1970, several prominent San Francisco area companies, including Standard Oil, the Bechtel Corporation, and Wells Fargo Bank, were so impressed with OAP's results they asked the organization to expand its services beyond alcoholism treatment and offer similar counseling to those suffering from a wide range of guilt-related symptoms, including burnout, workplace anger, and other forms of substance abuse. OAP eventually changed its name to Employee Assistance Professionals (EAP) and, by 2008, had an estimated three thousand counselors in thirty-five countries. It also inspired comparable programs in other parts of the world, such as Australia and New Zealand's Inter-Church Trade and Ministry Mission.

Clean When Washed

The unexpected leniency in the spiritual requirement to make amends for past misdeeds is that the reward does not depend on whether the gesture is accepted or visibly appreciated. For while the person who was harmed is not always in a forgiving mood and resists any attempt to make things right, the lack of pardon, while disappointing, does not diminish the healing power of the act. "We are clean when we are washed," as the University of Wisconsin's John Bascom (1874–1887) liked to put it, even "though the anointing oil is not extended to us."[188]

A hostile or even lukewarm reception may just mean the person receiving the apology needs time for the offering to sink in. Feelings of hurt and betrayal do not dissipate easily. And, even when they do recede, they are not always followed by a restoration of trust.

In reaction to such a negative reception, it is important the amends not be diluted with a self-serving justification or qualification, such as: "I'm sorry I hurt you, but if you hadn't hurt me first, I wouldn't have done it." The original Greek word for apology (*apologeisthai*) translates to "a strong defense" or "to speak in one's defense," which suggests just how easily one is tempted to not suffer the judgment of an injured party.

But even if honest atonement is never wholeheartedly accepted, the apology still transforms the person who offered it, not only relieving his or her sense of guilt but initiating a thoroughgoing change in his or her social and emotional environment. Indeed, so profound is the transformation that third parties with no relationship to the one who was harmed respond to it, often seeming friendlier and, if they are colleagues at the office, easier to work with. Even longstanding family conflicts begin to lose their edge.

The "instant you are genuinely sorry and ashamed, and resolved to renounce it," wrote Bowdoin president William DeWitt Hyde (1885–1917), "...the fetters of inhumanity drop from your limbs; and you stand up a free man, clothed not in the inhumanity you despise, but in the humanity you admire and strive to become."[189] Other people, he explained, sense the inner transformation and respond accordingly. One's own memory of the misdeed lingers as a caution not to repeat it, but the capacity to live harmoniously in God's universe has been restored.

It is especially important to know that this final "clean" phase will come, lest one be tempted to forsake amends and settle for some kind of self-punishment—as if any human could actually play God with oneself: comprehending all the reasons for the original misdeed, knowing its importance in the cosmic scheme of things, and logically determining the right price to be paid. Unfortunately, the current social climate, in which candidates for political office jump mercilessly on every flaw in their opponents' backgrounds, gives seeming credence to the idea that having done something wrong in the past is grounds for calculable punishment.

Scripture is clear: "If we confess our sins, he is faithful and just to forgive us *our* sins, and to cleanse us from all unrighteousness." (1 *John* 1:9) Any attempt to demand more of ourselves than the situation demands only denies God the benefit of our ongoing service.

If Christ's two overriding commandments are "love the Lord thy God with all thy heart, and with all thy soul, and with all thy mind" and to "love thy neighbour as thyself" (*Matthew* 22:37–39), it is hard to see where self-punishment fits in. Dwelling on already-confessed sins does not help us love Him more. Nor does it help us love other people more.

It is not a coincidence one of today's most respected parenting experts, Joanna Faber, author of *How to Talk So Little Kids Will Listen*, has said the most effective way to prepare a child for a healthy adulthood is to encourage him or her to admit and promptly rectify mistakes. "The best way to inspire a child to do better in the future is to give him an opportunity to do better in the present," she writes. "Making amends helps him feel good about himself, and helps him to see himself as a person who can do good."[190]

The Grace of God

Sadly, there are times when making adequate amends for a long-ago transgression is not possible—most obviously when the injured person has moved to parts unknown, become mentally incompetent, or perhaps has died. It is also possible even the most sensitively contemplated apology still promises to cause more harm than good, compounding whatever damage has already been done.

Consider two contrasting cases. The first involves Mark, a businessman who for years has been cheating on the company expense account, writing off his frequent visits to the racetrack as client entertainment. The accumulated guilt has become unbearable and now he wants to clear his conscience—but how? He might confess to pilfering the funds and offer to pay back what is owed. Or, if that seems too risky, he could just absorb the legitimate expenses of future business trips from his own pocket until the amount has been repaid. Either way is possible, and there are likely other solutions as well.

But now take the very different situation of a woman who years ago slept with her best friend's husband. How much good would be accomplished by coming clean today? Or what about the person who once committed a serious criminal act with the help of now-reformed accomplices, whose own lives and families might be greatly disrupted by the revelation?

The early college presidents were quick to insist that any decision to make one's amends should, as Yale College president Noah Porter put it, "abound with all judgment"[191] and not offend against good manners, become excessively obtrusive, impatient, or in any way destructive. As it says in 2 *Timothy* 2:24, the servant of the Lord must "be gentle unto all *men*."

If making amends directly to the person harmed is neither possible nor prudent, one can still pray to God directly, confessing the sin, repenting the transgression, and asking for His forgiveness. This was a great legacy of Christ's mission on Earth: to lift the emotional burden from souls who recognize the damage they have caused and would willingly do right by a person they have harmed, but no longer have the means to do so.

For critics of faith, the mystery of how this happens has always been a favorite target—their argument being so great a blessing could never be so readily available. Yet rigorous studies of the subject have sided firmly with the promises of Scripture.

In 2003, two researchers, Neal Krause from the University of Michigan and Christopher G. Ellison with University of Texas, divided a large group of senior citizens into two groups: those who at some point sought God's forgiveness for past misdeeds and those who had not. As it turned out, people in the first group reported much higher satisfaction with the quality of their lives and fewer symptoms of psychiatric problems, especially depression. Interestingly, those who made their amends to God also developed a more magnanimous attitude toward humanity in general. They were two and a half times more likely to believe all sinners should be forgiven unconditionally than those who had not sought Divine forgiveness.[192]

In 2007, psychologist Kelly McConnell and her colleagues at Bowling Green State University wrote "Transgression and Transformation," a summary of all the research up to that date on spiritual approaches to guilt. Not only did they find seeking God's pardon significantly reduces feelings of remorse, but it also has the unexpected effect of making Him seem more caring. People who had thought God judgmental and impatient before petitioning His pardon reported a far more loving concept afterwards.[193]

It is findings such as these which have led doctors at Duke University and at the Charlie Norwood VA Medical Center in Augusta, Georgia, to collaborate in the use of spiritual treatment of veterans with Post-Traumatic Stress Disorder (PTSD). While medicine alone helps some patients reduce the number of nightmares and flashbacks, and psychotherapy appears to benefit others, about a third do not respond to either approach.

Neither of these conventional therapies "addresses moral injury and inner conflict," notes Dr. Nagy Youssef, lead scientist on the project. "Somebody goes to combat, seeing friends being killed and killing others. Spirituality might be affected. It might go against their moral beliefs. That's hard to reconcile when they come back."[194]

Modern psychology may not yet be exactly on the same page as America's early college presidents, but with the efforts of researchers like Dr. Youssef, it keeps getting closer.

Reflection:

*If we confess our sins, He is faithful and
just to forgive us our sins, and to cleanse
us from all unrighteousness.*
—1 John *1:9*

LESSON EIGHT:

ELEVATE DAILY ENCOUNTERS

The same qualities, the same conditions, the same means—not different—are required for relation to God and relation to men, though we have been singularly slow in recognizing it.

> —Henry Churchill King, president
> of Oberlin College (1902–1927)[195]

The Kingdom of God is the realm of companionships.... Lives are born to bring them into fellowship with other lives.

> —Francis John McConnell, president
> of DePauw University (1909–1912)[196]

So far as God acts upon us and for us, he acts largely through social agencies. These forces and these laws act upon us through their relations to

ourselves and to others.... The spirit of the living
God not only dwells in each single soul to make
it a temple for worship and service, but it brings
them together into a spiritual organism, which it
molds for a dwelling-place for himself, inspiring
each single agency with new energy, and lifting all
together into a higher, common life.

—*Noah Porter, president of*
Yale College (1871–1886)[197]

The Essence of Failure

Like most other early college presidents, William Rainey Harper
(1891–1906) was dedicated to improving education both
on campus and off. Not only did he found and preside over
the University of Chicago during the late nineteenth century,
Harper started the first agricultural extension service to provide
Midwestern farmers with modern techniques for improving crop
yields and expanding their herds. He also established the nation's
first ever sociology department and invented the prototype for
what would become America's community college system.

Yet Harper's biographer, Albion Small, describes a man who
was never so busy he failed to treat everyone he met, from his
barber to his state's Congressmen, as if they too had an important
mission with "a place to fill and part to perform." His friendships
included not just the famous and influential, but local shopkeepers, restaurant waiters, and even his university's janitors.

Indeed, Harper's most characteristic expression upon learning someone found a new interest was, "Oh, how I wish I could drop everything and give myself to that!"[198] And whenever he heard a colleague complaining of feeling discouraged, Harper invariably advised him to become more involved in the lives of his friends and neighbors.

Picture the man who has become truly bored, he once said, someone whose life has become "fixed," "hardened," and "impervious to influence," someone who feels himself bored or stuck in a groove. "What element in the true policy of life does this man lack, or what element does he possess that makes his life a failure?" Has he not, in the end, lost interest in "other souls?"[199]

Harper was hardly alone in this conviction. The importance of never taking others for granted is a powerful theme in the biographies of many early American college presidents. Timothy Dwight IV, who led Yale College from 1795 to 1817, was famous throughout New England for the number and strength of his friendships. Dwight's acquaintances, said his biographer John Trumbull, "revered and loved him most." Trumbull attributed this fact to the Yale president's lifetime habit of listening carefully to other people's problems and never thinking himself superior to anyone else, even when a controversial belief or criminal conviction rendered a friend an object "of reproach and calumny" in the community.[200]

And of Wesleyan president Bradford P. Raymond, who served from 1889 to 1908, it was often said he dealt as warmly with strangers on the street as he did the most celebrated personalities of his day. "There was nothing harsh, censorious, arrogant, about the man," remembered the school's English professor, Caleb Winchester. "In the twenty-seven years I knew him, I never heard him say a single malicious or contemptuous word of any man."[201]

Even Duke's notoriously introspective Braxton Craven, who could sometimes get so lost in his thoughts he seemed oblivious to passersby, nevertheless took time from his busy schedule to arbitrate neighborhood disputes, help local farmers with his knowledge of agriculture, take in poor students as boarders, and visit small churches of various denominations throughout the region. Indeed, without the goodwill Craven built throughout North Carolina, it is unlikely Duke could have survived either its unusual founding as a hybrid Methodist–Quaker college or the economic collapse of a defeated South after the Civil War.

Today we are likely to dismiss the outgoing demeanor of a university president as the polished façade of a professional fundraiser, but this impression is a radical change from earlier times when the leaders of Christian colleges were notoriously contemptuous of what they called "financial promotion." (A good school's reputation, they believed, should speak for itself.) The extra measure of respect that Dwight, Raymond, Craven, and the other presidents showed their fellow creatures stemmed entirely from their appreciation of *New Testament* chronology, which does not end with a final account of Jesus's life and teachings, nor with the *Acts* of the Apostles and its proclamation of salvation through Christ, or with the *Epistles* and their description of the emerging church. Scripture concludes instead with the *Revelation of St. John*, wherein it is prophesied Jesus will have a final victory over His enemies and all the saints will gather in celebration of one community—a city of God.

This prediction, the presidents believed, is on one level a promise about the future. But it is also a subtle critique of the widely shared delusion that much of social life is random and unimportant, a series of unavoidable interruptions on the way to more pressing business. Sure, we tell ourselves, there is always the occasional situation that demands we stop and render aid to a stranger in distress. No one questions why Christ held up the example of the Good Samaritan, who helped the Jewish businessman injured by robbers and bought him medicine and lodging at a nearby inn. (*Luke* 10:25–37) But few encounters are ever serious enough to demand our attention.

In fact, the presidents said, there is no such thing as an accidental meeting with another soul—for every human encounter, no matter how unplanned or temporary it might appear, occurs for a reason. As Mount Holyoke Female Seminary president Mary Lyon (1837–1849) so often reminded her students, God makes His wishes known, not only in the privacy of the intuitive mind but, "through the agency of man."[202] The people who appear in our lives at each moment are, as she put it, "pre-positioned" for our spiritual development, just as we have a role to play in theirs.

It is not an exaggeration to say the early college presidents regarded all their interactions as no less than Divinely-arranged appointments, never to be taken for granted or regarded as inconsequential but honored as a possible context for something grander than circumstances suggest. Therefore, to treat other people as mere props or conveniences was to disrespect the Lord himself. Conversely, to act as if each person one met had a soul, consciously or unconsciously in God's service, enables the moment to unfold to its highest purpose.

And, while this highest purpose could never be fully known, the mere fact of regarding all encounters as Divinely arranged elevates the overall quality of life, making every hour, every place, and every event more special than it would otherwise appear. When each human interaction is dealt with as a spiritual opportunity, Colgate College president Ebenezer Dodge (1868–1890) told his students, then "every duty has a Divine blessing." A subtle joyfulness pervades daily life, challenging the aristocracy of what the secular world deems to be uniquely superior events, positions, honors, and careers.[203]

Trifles of Manner

A wonderful psychological achievement in any age, if we had a clear idea of how to engineer it, but what exactly did the presidents mean by treating every encounter as a "Divinely-arranged appointment?" Does this require some special ritual or form of address? A certain way of speaking? Does even a fleeting stranger have to be spiritually acknowledged?

The presidents would often begin to answer such questions with the Scriptural account of a prominent Shunammite woman who, upon hearing the prophet Elisha was passing nearby, persuades him to stop, rest, and eat some bread she baked. Her generosity was not motivated by the desire for some favor or to improve her image in the community, only the opportunity to be hospitable. Grateful for the unexpected meal and aware of the woman's good intentions, Elisha remembered her kindness and "*so* it was, *that* as oft as he passed by, he turned in thither to eat bread." (2 *Kings* 4:8)

What the presidents took from this passage is respect for others is often best expressed, not in flowery speech or grand gestures, but in common courtesies: the extra moment taken to inquire of another's health, the acknowledgement of an apparent need, or the effort made to follow up on a previous conversation.

"A reverent love for another shows itself in trifles of manner," president Henry Churchill King (1902–1927) instructed his Oberlin College students. "And our love to Christ will best show itself in similar care in the trifles of our daily life. We make no sacrifice so great as that which manifests itself in what we count the small things of daily living."

The chief mark of a spiritual attitude toward others, King was saying, often lies "in the slighter things." The "cup of cold water given in the name of a disciple, Christ assures us, is taken as given directly to him. And if one finds he is always having his own way, however smoothly and graciously that may seem to be occurring, he may well suspect that he is guilty of real selfishness."[204]

To the modern mind, taking care of the "trifles" undoubtedly sounds a bit old fashioned—so much so that many would immediately dismiss the prescription. "Isn't it healthier for people in need to speak up for themselves?" today's sophisticate would argue. This stylish pronouncement might well be followed with, "Who am I to impose on somebody else's life?" Or, "Isn't it possible always being courteous to others just puts an unfair burden on them to be excessively polite in return?"

I must confess to holding similar views myself for many years. Not that I skimped on writing the periodic check to charity or lacked trendy causes to support. But like so many other nominal Christians, I would nod in mechanical agreement with my pastor's Sunday sermons about good fellowship and caring for my brother, but I never really considered what that meant on a day-to-day level. The thought of taking an extra beat to comment on an acquaintance's worried expression, or to ask after the health of someone he or she once introduced me to, rarely crossed my mind.

That is, until one Sunday a few weeks after my youngest child went off to college. I was attending church by myself in the same sanctuary where my late wife and I had raised our two children, when it came to the familiar point in the service where the minister asks the congregation to rise and greet those in nearby pews. It was then I realized I did not actually know any of the people approaching to shake my hand.

It was not that I had never seen or spoken to them before—our family had attended that same church for nearly twenty years. But almost everything I did during that time was something either my wife or I believed important for our children's religious educations: escorting them to confirmation class, helping them dress for the Christmas pageant, and attending the occasional after-service seminar. Not only had I found ways to keep my contribution to these tasks to a minimum (without appearing to be doing so, of course), but even while involved in church activities, my mind was often elsewhere.

It was not until this first Sunday alone when it finally struck me: the people I sped by for so many years were not just random Christian extras drawn from nearby towns; rather, on a deeper spiritual level, they were my closest spiritual companions. All of us were believers who not only prayed daily for God's guidance but made the effort to do so weekly in the same location; yet I was hard pressed to even recall many of their names.

It was a humiliating realization—one which made me see that, for all my intellectual interest in religion and spiritual growth, I regularly glossed over the very people in my life whose beliefs were the closest to my own.

In the following months, it was a revelation to discover just how much my Sundays brightened as I extended myself to other churchgoers in small but respectful ways: remembering to follow up on a joy or concern someone announced to the congregation during a previous service, volunteering to help our busy pastor track down a guest speaker he wanted for the weekly adult education class, or making sure a handicapped parishioner was not ignored at the fellowship hour after services.

Arthur Brooks, the head of a well-known economics think tank, tells a similar story in a 2016 guest editorial he wrote for the *Wall Street Journal*. Brooks recalls how his own life was changed by the funeral of his father, where literally hundreds of mourners showed up. Dutifully going from one person to the next to ask what he or she most appreciated about his father, Brooks was stunned when nearly everyone responded with the same phrase: "He was a very nice man."

"Not a bad legacy," Brooks thought to himself. And so, to the chagrin of his own children, he set out to imitate a few of his father's social habits, especially the tendency to stop and initiate a cheerful exchange with a passing stranger. These friendly gestures, he freely admits, were not always reciprocated; but the practice truly "made me a happier person."[205]

Interestingly, there have even been two scientific studies on the emotional effect of what the presidents called "attending to the trifles." The first, conducted by British researchers in 2010 and published in the *Journal of Social Psychology*, showed that people who take the trouble to be unusually helpful and understanding of others are significantly happier than those who do not.[206]

The second, conducted by Gillian Sandstrom, a senior lecturer in the Department of Psychology at England's University of Essex, asked participants to exchange simple pleasantries with one stranger a day for five days. The overwhelming majority (99 percent) of those who did said they found at least one of the conversations surprisingly pleasant, 82 percent said they learned something interesting from at least one of the strangers, 43 percent ended up actually exchanging contact information, and 40 percent followed up enough that they seemed to be making new friends.

Dr. Sandstrom's research has shown that people's moods greatly improve when they go out of their way to connect with passersby and are happier when they interact more often with casual acquaintances. Those who make such efforts, she says, end up feeling "like they are part of something bigger."[207]

But perhaps the most persuasive experimental evidence for attending to the trifles comes from our own recollection of how it feels when someone we've hardly met has nevertheless taken the trouble to remember our name. Instantly, we feel more valued and more desirous of reciprocating the compliment. That is exactly how relative strangers react every time we take the trouble to treat their presence as more than a random coincidence.

Benjamin Franklin's Example

And if ennobling our daily encounters requires us to better attend to the "trifles," the presidents argued, it also requires us to treat everyone we meet with a certain humility, even if we must occasionally force it. As it says in *Proverbs* 29:23, "A man's pride shall bring him low: but honour shall uphold the humble in spirit."

Many of the early college presidents like to tell the *Old Testament* story of King Nebuchadnezzar, the unhappy ruler of ancient Babylon whose delusions of grandeur led him to regard every person he met as an inferior. "Be careful," his Hebrew counselor Daniel finally warned the king in so many words, when asked to interpret one of the king's anxious nightmares. "If you persist with this attitude," Daniel explained, "you will only make yourself more miserable. Like some animal isolated in the fields, you will become depressed—and remain so until you have recognized only God is entitled to hold himself above others." Unfortunately for Nebuchadnezzar, it took seven more years until he was desperate enough to heed Daniel's advice and begin exercising deliberate humility.

Even more than King Nebuchadnezzar, nineteenth-century college presidents liked to point to a famously formative incident from the early life of Benjamin Franklin. It was a persuasive example, not only of the connection between humility and the quality of a person's worldly associations, but of the fact even someone not naturally disposed to modesty could nevertheless benefit from forcing the appearance of it.

The year was 1730, and Franklin was still a struggling young printer in Philadelphia. He accepted the invitation of a local minister to attend a series of sermons on morality but was so put off by the cleric's boring presentation he soon decided to stop going.

Yet the subject of intentional character improvement continued to fascinate Franklin and he eventually got the idea for what many presidents considered the New World's very first psychology experiment. He decided to make a list of all the personality traits most people regard as good or admirable—sincerity, temperance, frugality, and so on—and then systematically practice each one for several days to see what effect it might have on his life. "I made," he later recalled, "a little book, in which I allotted a page for each of the virtues…. I determined to give a week's strict attention to each…marking every evening the faults of the day."[208]

Unsurprisingly in Franklin's case, the trait of modesty was not even on his original list. It was only because he outlined the project to a Quaker acquaintance, who promptly told Franklin he was generally thought arrogant and self-centered, that "humility" was added at the last minute. "[The Quaker] kindly informed me," he remembered, "that I was generally thought proud; that my pride showed itself frequently in conversation; that I was not content with being in the right when discussing any point, but was overbearing and rather insolent."

Equally unsurprising was the fact humility turned out to be an especially difficult virtue for Franklin to master, at least in the beginning. His first efforts were so stumbling and inconsistent that Franklin found he had to make it a hard "rule to forebear all direct contradiction to the sentiments of others," even expressions "that imported a fix'd opinion, such as *certainly, undoubtedly,* and so on."

When he did render an opinion, Franklin forced himself to couple it with a modifying phrase such as "I conceive," "I apprehend," "I imagine," or "so appears to me at present." It was only with some effort what he "at first put on with some violence to natural inclination" became at length much easier.

Yet looking back on this self-experiment in later years, Franklin had to admit it was his willingness to literally force himself to be (or at least sound) humble which, more than anything else, was responsible for the respect and affection he elicited throughout the rest of his life. "And to this habit...I think it principally owing," he wrote, "that I had early so much weight with my fellow citizens...and so much influence in public councils when I became a member."

True, Franklin's arrogance never completely disappeared in the privacy of his mind. No matter how much he might "disguise it, struggle with it, beat it down, stifle it, [or] mortify it," his pride would "every now and then peep out and show itself." But at least he learned when to hold his tongue, and that seemed to be sufficient.

Speaking about our own time, it is not a coincidence that thoughtful therapists so often prescribe enforced humility as the remedy for troubled relationships. For the late Dr. M. Scott Peck, author of many books on the link between spiritual values and mental health, a client he called Betsy illustrated the cure especially well. A lovely and intelligent twenty-two-year-old, she appeared on the surface to have everything.[209]

"My husband is good to me," she told Peck in their first session. "We love each other very much." Yet privately Betsy suffered from feelings of isolation so intense not even the powerful tranquilizers she was taking could relieve her anxiety.

Betsy started therapy putting all the blame on her husband. His manners were "uncouth," she said. His interests were too narrow, and he watched too much TV. But as treatment progressed, it became clear Betsy's real problem was her own judgmental habit, which kept her from feeling close to others. Years before, she quit college because she felt superior to classmates who were "into drugs and sex a lot." She also didn't approve of people who questioned the church or her family's values. She may have thought herself a good Christian, but by consistently imagining herself superior to others, she effectively walled out the joys of everyday living.

The late Dr. Thomas Hora is another highly regarded Christian psychiatrist whose approach to treating loneliness was remarkably like the early college presidents' prescription for elevating daily encounters. He was especially influenced by the fact patients who complained the most about being bored with life or feeling isolated from others were those with the most condescending attitudes.[210]

"Isn't it interesting," Hora once wrote, "that we start out criticizing other people to make ourselves feel better. And the more we do this, the worse we are going to feel, because if we criticize others, we [build up]…a burdensome load of thoughts which we don't want anyone to know. Consequently, the more we try to feel better the worse we feel. This is the way one cripples oneself socially. It becomes more and more difficult to communicate with one's fellow men and participate in the social process."[211]

In other words, the adage "if you can't say anything nice, don't say anything at all" turns out to be a profound piece of therapeutic wisdom. It is perhaps for this reason there are more maxims in Scripture, including *Proverbs* 21:33, along the lines of watch your mouth and tongue than any other subject.

For someone trying to curtail a critical habit, it is important to understand that speaking less does not isolate oneself even more. Not only do other people appreciate having a greater say over the direction of a conversation, but they intuitively sense a connection between brevity and wisdom. "Even a fool, when he holdeth his peace, is counted wise: *and* he that shutteth his lips *is esteemed* a man of understanding." (*Proverbs* 17:28)

The intelligence implied by speaking less is perhaps most famously reflected in the introduction to a 1657 letter written by the French mathematician and philosopher Blaise Pascal. "I have made this longer than usual," he started, "because I have not had time to make it shorter."

A Surprising Experiment

If punctuating our day with gestures of kindness—and doing so humbly—opens the door to a more satisfying life, it is by risking ever-greater honesty, the early college presidents believed, that we maximize the spiritual benefit. It is not that we must be completely and loquaciously frank at every moment but, when at the point of not knowing how far to go, we must venture just a bit beyond our comfort zone.

Case Western Reserve University president Charles F. Thwing (1890–1921) called this attitude "standing at the point of truthfulness." If this is your approach to others, he once wrote, "you will find that your own being will become great in its truthfulness…. Truth magnifies the man searching for, finding, holding, and expressing it."[212]

Taking incremental risks to be more open is admittedly a difficult spiritual challenge in today's world. We live in an exceptionally mobile time, when so many of the people we meet at work, in the neighborhood, and even at church are not very well-known to us. Who are they really? Where did they come from, and how likely is it they might abuse a confidence for selfish or even malicious reasons?

In such a time, we all have a protective tendency to blunt our spiritual powers, not with great lies and exaggerations but with subtle misstatements or by letting what we know to be inaccuracies stand uncorrected. How often do we imagine we are safer withholding an uncomfortable truth or by allowing others to proceed along misinformed lines?

The late nineteenth and early twentieth century Christian college presidents anticipated our problem. They could see how the increasingly rapid pace of technological progress was making it all too easy for their undergraduates to breeze past each other, treating fellow classmates with no more thought than what was temporarily good for themselves. Many, like the University of Chicago's Harper, organized campus talks specifically to remind students of the need to treat everyday interactions as much more than the superficial encounters they appear to be.[213]

Taking the risk to be more available to others, the presidents were quick to add, does not mean telling your life story to everyone you meet. Neither does it mean answering questions that seem painfully or inappropriately invasive. When uncomfortably pressed, it is perfectly fine to say, "I don't feel comfortable discussing that right now," "I'd rather not get into it today," or "I'd rather not say." But being sensibly protective should never allow us to forget every person is a living soul, connected even if unconsciously to God. And if one wishes to transcend the material world, self-imposed barriers to greater intimacy must be constantly challenged.

Spiritual growth may not have been on the mind of University of Connecticut psychologist Julian Rotter when, in 1980, he designed a study to find out what happens to those who risk trusting others, but the results were nonetheless telling.[214] Rotter decided to develop what he called an "Interpersonal Trust Scale," a series of statements which, taken together, measured a person's openness toward others.

For example, someone who agreed "people are more hypocritical than ever" would be considered less trusting in his or her outlook, while a person who thought washing machine repairmen "are honest" would get a higher score. Rotter would then administer his scale to groups of undergraduate volunteers and compare their scores with tests designed to reveal the quality of their everyday social lives.

Many colleagues who had heard of Rotter's planned study undoubtedly thought it a waste of a good researcher's time. Surely the more trusting subject would be exposed as foolishly naïve and proven to be surrounded by fair-weather companions who likely took advantage of him. And while the caution of the distrusters might leave them with fewer friends, at least they would be the kind of people one could more reliably depend upon.

Undaunted, Rotter went ahead with his research and, in the end, found the very opposite of what the cynics anticipated. As it turned out, the more open a subject was willing to be, the more he or she attracted acquaintances very much like oneself—honest and forthcoming. Similarly, the habitual distrusters also attracted reflections of themselves, people who tended to be secretive, manipulative, and disloyal.

In his formal write-up of the project, Rotter had to concede there is something far more profound than generally realized to the saying "you get out of life what you put into it." Those who take the risk to be more open with others elicit a complementary response from those willing to do the same, while circumspection attracts only those who themselves are reluctant to be forthcoming.[215] It was a conclusion not all that different from the spiritual prescription preached by America's early college presidents: in relationships, most people respond in kind to what they are offered—frankness with frankness, deceit with deceit.

In the years since Rotter's original study, research has shown those who take the risk to be more honest not only have a more rewarding social life, but superior health with which to enjoy it. The willingness to be open with others tends to lower blood pressure, the risk of diabetes, and even the likelihood of heart disease. "The physical world of our bodies gets remodeled by our psychic and conceptual worlds," UCLA researcher Steven Cole has observed; and even a slightly more honest approach to others can have significant healthful effects.[216] There is also experimental evidence that those who are more trusting are also more energetic and alert, as well as less anxious.[217]

Nice Guys Finish First

Being sensitive to the need for small comforts, restraining pride, and venturing greater openness: this is not the prescription for happiness one is likely to find in a contemporary self-help book, but it is one that does, in fact, have a profound and lasting influence on the character of everyday life.

As Oberlin College president Henry Churchill King (1902–1927) argued a century ago in books like *Fundamental Questions* and *The Seeming Unreality of the Spiritual Life*, the single-minded pursuit of celebrity, power, or professional status may yield fleeting pleasures, but what truly transforms the world, both within and without, is the refusal to treat others as mere scenery. "The decision for which life calls is the decision between the determination to seek the larger life," he wrote, and the willingness to remain content with "the lesser good" of superficial relationships.[218]

Or as Stanford University's founding president David Starr Jordan (1891–1913) once observed, human fulfillment is a matter of proximity, not ambition. "The nearest," he said, "is the greatest in most human lives."[219] It is by elevating our daily encounters that we experience the best our brief time on Earth has to offer.

What almost every contemporary self-help book does seem to recommend to each of us is developing "a more balanced life"—as if satisfaction were a function of how evenly we divide our time among work, family, friends, entertainment, and volunteer activities. This is an especially curious prescription from Christian writers, as few Biblical exemplars, male or female, ever led what could be called a "balanced life."

Consider Ruth the Moabite who, widowed young, resolved first to protect her mother-in-law and then follow God's will for the rest of her days, wherever it led. Or Mary Magdalene who, after being healed by Jesus, traveled as far as she could with Him, witnessing his crucifixion, burial, and resurrection. And, of course, both Peter and Paul undertook a long series of arduous and dangerous journeys in order to establish the early church. Nowhere does Scripture suggest that these, or any of the other admirable figures it memorializes, were too single-minded.

If there is any equilibrium we should be striving for, it is not between the separate compartments of our lives, but between the opportunities available to each moment. After all, how can we best serve God if we insist on ignoring the very people and situations He keeps trying to introduce us to?

Reflection:

Finally, be ye all of one mind,
having compassion one of another, love as
brethren, be pitiful, be courteous....
—1 Peter 3:8

EXPECT MOODINESS AND DISCONTENT

There lives not a man who is always free from inward conflict. It may seem to be transitory; but it is nevertheless there, deep and abiding in the soul. It is in this condition of disquiet and unrest that the Savior's invitation comes to us, and his promise meets our conscious wants. Come unto me, and I will give you rest.

—Lewis W. Green, president of Hampden–Sydney College (1848 –1856)[220]

Let things flow or ebb, the chain will hold to the anchor. The promises will not ravel. Somber hours, like some birds of dingiest plumage, will burst into the brightest carol. The harvests need the night as

*well as the day to ripen them. It takes the whole
quartet of the seasons to utter the fugal year.*

—Melancthon Woolsey Stryker, president
of Hamilton College (1892–1917) [221]

*The man who is willing to let his course be decided
in every case by his passing mood has evidently
given up any rational guidance of his life. He
may boast himself of his freedom, but he is really
a slave of his circumstances; for the feeling which
he allows to determine his course is the immediate
response to the circumstances. The man for whom
it is sufficient reason always to say "I don't feel like
it," thereby gives up a man's life, and accepts the
destiny of a chip on the waters.*

—Henry Churchill King, president
of Oberlin College (1902–1927)[222]

The City of God

Of all the ancient Christian teachers, the early college presidents had a special affection for Augustine of Hippo, better known today as Saint Augustine. Born in 354 AD near Carthage in Northern Africa, he grew up an unusually ambitious man who, in his late twenties, set sail across the Mediterranean to make a name for himself in Rome.

From there, he moved to the empire's capital in Milan, where his literary talents were recognized, and he was soon appointed a professor of public speaking at the city university. With commissions to write speeches for the Emperor, his recent advantageous engagement to a wealthy heiress, and a mistress on the side, Augustine was on the verge of achieving all the worldly success any aspiring pagan of the time could want, when an unexpected religious conversion in a small garden changed everything.

Retreating briefly with a small group of Christians to the harbor city of Ostia outside Rome, Augustine eventually returned home to Northern Africa where he sold the farm he inherited from his parents, used some of the proceeds to start a small monastery, and distributed the rest to the poor. After that, he went on to write some of the most influential books in the history of Western civilization.

One of the traits the early college presidents undoubtedly found so appealing about Augustine was his sensitivity, even before his conversion, to the emotional price of letting his ambition trump his values. There is a particularly poignant passage in his autobiography, where he recalls what it felt like to prepare a speech in praise of the Emperor, knowing full well his facts were either made up or wildly distorted. Walking later that evening along the streets of Milan, trying to justify to himself what he earlier wrote, he noticed a drunken beggar across the road, laughing uncontrollably and talking out loud. Contrasting their two conditions, his own mind so troubled and the beggar so cheerfully carefree, Augustine finally burst out, "Will I never cease setting my heart on shadows and following a lie?"[223]

Once converted to Christianity, it would have been tempting for Augustine to withdraw completely from society and compose his great books in some location where he would not have to deal with pagan values and customs. But as time went by, he found himself becoming far more involved in civic affairs than he ever was in Milan—hearing and settling disputes among his neighbors, traveling widely to defend the young Christian religion against its many detractors, and preaching more than 350 sermons across the Mediterranean world. As cynical and corrupt as the Roman Empire was becoming, Augustine's understanding of his newfound faith told him there is always a way for the true believer to serve God in the public square, be it in the arts, education, commerce, music, or even city administration.

Anticipating the early college presidents' belief in the desirability of expressing God's will through, not isolated from, the workaday world, Augustine responded to the eventual news of Rome's fall by spending the next seventeen years on his greatest work, *The City of God*. In it, he argued that however materialistically corrupt the larger society might become, it at least provided the faithful with enough peace and order to follow their callings. It was an idea that had a powerful influence on both the Renaissance and the European Enlightenment, reaching its fullest expression in the colonization of North America and the founding of the United States.

"No earthly enjoyment can compensate."

The biggest drawback to a worldly calling, Augustine understood, is that one's joy in serving God is tempered by the pressures to take material reality more seriously than one would like: the need to engage in contingency planning, to be accountable to one's commitments regardless the current mood, and to communicate in ways non-believers can understand. Every self-identified soul must contend with the paradox that the more flexibility a civilization provides to follow God's direction, the more challenging it becomes to cope with the appearances civilization mistakes for reality.

It was a theme taken up often by American college presidents, who clearly believed the more opportunity a free and prosperous society offers to follow one's calling, the less satisfying the world can sometimes seem. "You [will frequently] feel that there is something unsatisfying in these very comforts and enjoyments of yours," James McCosh warned Princeton's graduating seniors during his two decades as the school's president (1868–1888). "The eye is not satisfied with seeing, nor the ear with hearing, nor ambition with success, nor the lust with gratification. Ay, there is something wanting, and you know it; you feel it at times, though you may not yet know what it is that would fill the void."[224]

Like another famous nineteenth-century college president, Yale's Theodore Woolsey (1846–1871), McCosh knew this want of enjoyment "for which no earthly enjoyment can compensate"[225] is just as likely to occur in the best of times as in the worst. Even when one's personal and career dreams seem to be coming true and there is not a financial or health-related cloud in the sky.

Nothing so ill-prepares people for the spiritual life, early college leaders knew, than the idealized image of the deeply religious person as always unruffled, no matter what the circumstances. Not only is every Christian subject to chronic discontent, but also to the allure of escapist fantasies which rush in to fill an emotional void—the desire to flee one's work and domestic obligations, to have an affair, to jolt one's consciousness (with drugs, overeating, or gambling), to vent a pent-up resentment, or even to adopt a new identity. It was the inability to wait out his own discontent that led King David to seduce the wife of his loyal soldier Uriah, the prophet Elijah to flee the pressures of being a high-profile seer, and even Moses to rebel against the long wilderness exodus by striking the rock at Meribah.

Like every other early president, the University of Chicago's William Rainey Harper (1891–1906) tried to reassure undergraduates that their own bouts of restless dissatisfaction were perfectly normal and would, in fact, return at the most unexpected times. "To every life there will come [these] hours," he would say, but feelings of moodiness and discontent are no judgment on how well anyone has lived. "Many times, the man who, as the world thinks, has achieved great success will feel with Macbeth 'the wine of life is drawn and the mere lees is left this vault to brag of.'"[226]

We Need Polishing

The good news, as Augustine observed, is that the experience of discontent is not entirely negative. Far more than an unavoidable inconvenience—the unpleasant side effect of living spiritually in an imperfect world—disgruntlement is a state God often uses to capture our attention. It is His way of breaking through our habitual view of the world to gift us with a deeper perspective, to help us solve a problem, or perhaps to alert us to a new service.

"The deeper we go in the valley, the higher God intends to raise us towards the mountaintop," DePauw University's Matthew Simpson (1839–1848) would remind his students. "God intends, as he sinks us in sorrow, to raise us in joy; and it is our privilege to rejoice evermore, and to know that all these trials are but blessings in another form."[227]

Simpson often compared moodiness and discontent to the shaping and polishing of precious gems. Had a diamond a consciousness, he would say, it would undoubtedly complain when put into a lathe. But when its rough edges were cut and from every angle a glorious light sparkled out, it would give thanks for that which gave it such power to shine. "It is so with us," he said. "On earth we need polishing—many of us; we must be put into the lathe…. God knows how much polishing we require, and when the work is performed he will [refrain]."[228]

More than a century later, when the Russian writer Aleksandr Solzhenitsyn was deported from the old Soviet Union and took up residence in the US, he expressed a similar sentiment, forcing his new countrymen to think deeply about their own lives. For six decades, he said, oppressive communist governments had put the people of Eastern Europe "through a spiritual training far in advance of Western experience." But in the case of those who suffered this "complex and deadly crush of life" with the right spiritual outlook, it produced "stronger deeper, and more interesting personalities than those generated by standardized Western well-being."[229]

Solzhenitsyn was not suggesting his newfound American friends would be better off by enduring a long political tyranny of their own, but he did think people in a free society were uniquely challenged to spiritually handle life's inevitable discontents. They had to voluntarily cultivate the ability to patiently endure—and even welcome as God's blessing—recurrent periods of restless dissatisfaction.[230]

Most contemporary psychologists do not speak in such overtly religious terms, but modern studies have long shown that tolerance for negative moods is highly correlated with personal creativity. An important "part of the creative process," admits Harvard University researcher Dr. Shelley Carson, "demands that we look at ourselves or our environment with some degree of dissatisfaction."[231]

Norwegian Business School Professor Geir Kaufmann, who has spent years studying the connection between mood and creativity, agrees with Carson. While it used to be thought negative emotions drained men and women of their artistic and inventive abilities, it now appears to be the opposite. "Deep thinking is related to sad moods," he says.[232]

Dr. Brian Lucas, who has studied creativity at both Northwestern University and the University of Chicago Booth School of Business, finds that people are most inventive at just the point where they have become disillusioned and doubt the value of their work. His advice to friends and colleagues who express discouragement is to ignore the mood as best they can and muster the energy to press on a bit further.[233] "Try to generate just a few more ideas," he says, "or consider just a few more alternatives. You may find that your next creative idea is closer than you imagined."

While researchers like Carson, Kaufmann, and Lucas are professionally constrained to account for the connection between mood and creativity in the terminology of contemporary science—

as a function of childhood conditioning, social setting or neural physiology—the spiritual understanding is no less valid: a mind sufficiently confident in God's guidance will not allow its dark moods to subvert what it intuits, however dimly, to be His calling.

Sow to the Spirit

As Hamilton College's Simeon North (1839–1857) so often warned his undergraduates, our inevitable bouts of dissatisfaction are often accompanied, not only by escapist fantasy, but by a paralytic skepticism—a tendency to dismiss one's inmost desires as "foolish," "trivial," "a waste of time," or "not good enough." And when we entertain such thinking long enough, we even begin to mistake it for intellectual sophistication, all the while becoming ever-more vulnerable to the kind of soft atheism described in Chapter Four. Like the fabled Tantalus, said North, we find ourselves longing for a renovating good that we somehow cannot grasp.[234]

Conversely, the more tenaciously we hold on to our apprehension of Divine purpose, what Mt. Holyoke Female Seminary president Mary Lyon (1837–1849) called "sowing to the spirit," the more quickly our experience will validate it. As difficult as it is to believe in our despairing moments, difficult effort does give way to excitement, frustration yields to gratification, and doubt dissolves into a more childlike spontaneity.[235]

Not surprisingly, Massachusetts Institute of Technology president Henry Pritchett (1900–1907) preferred a more scientific sounding metaphor, but his point was the same. You "will recall how imperfect is the transformation of energy, which is effected in the electric lamp," he would say to his budding electrical engineers. "We burn coal to make steam, and the energy thus generated by the heat is converted into mechanical energy, and this into electrical energy, and this finally into the energy of the light waves. The transformation in our individual hearts is akin to this process."

Just as much of nature's physical energy is lost in the translation of coal to light, Pritchett said, so much of a person's psychic energy is used up in dealing with life's ups and downs. "Only the remnant is left for transmutation into those things which are spiritual and eternal." But to the extent we dedicate whatever energy remains to God's service, "we become religious men. And in just such proportion as we succeed, in just such proportion do we realize that we are coming into relations with that God whom our fathers worshiped."[236]

Presidents Lyon and Pritchett were describing the kind of optimistic determination indicated in their own time with the word *grit*. It is a term recently revived by University of Pennsylvania psychologist Angela Lee Duckworth to describe her observation that what most characterizes people with rewarding lives is not IQ or talent, but the perseverance to realize one's heartfelt course when it is not so strongly heartfelt.

It is a conclusion she came to as far back as her first year in graduate school. That was when she managed to round up 164 eighth graders from a nearby middle school and give them all both traditional IQ tests and standard assessments of self-discipline. Over the course of the academic year she monitored each student's academic progress and then matched it to her earlier testing. To the surprise of the students' teachers, as well as to many of Duckworth's graduate school colleagues, the self-discipline scores turned out to be much better predictors of educational achievement success than IQ.[237]

What now intrigues Duckworth is the extent to which what she calls *grit* predicts many outcomes beyond secondary school. For example, people who score high in self-discipline get better grades in college, are less likely to get in trouble with the law, stay married longer, and are less likely to become substance abusers. In fact, she is hard-pressed to think of any desirable outcome grit does not make more probable.

When asked by a journalist to speculate on why her 2016 book *Grit: The Power of Passion and Perseverance* became so popular, especially with parents and teachers, Dr. Duckworth suggested society as a whole has become skeptical of standardized testing's ability to predict life satisfaction. Deep down, even many of her academic colleagues are coming back to the old-fashioned idea that long-term happiness comes from remaining faithful to one's inner calling, regardless of mood swings, periodic disappointments, and other distractions.[238] Not exactly how the Christian college presidents would have put it, but a lot closer than academic psychology has been for almost a century.

The Half-Ripe Stage

It is not a coincidence, the presidents thought, Scripture so often compares the course of a believer's calling to patterns in nature that punctuate moments of great beauty with less attractive junctures: a frail blade of grass in the spring pushing up from the soil or the fruit tree between the time the blossom has fallen and the reaping of a golden harvest.

This is God's way of saying that one's green and bitter phases are just as important as any other, although the worldly human mind cannot appreciate this. "He hath made every *thing* beautiful in his time: also he hath set the world in their heart, so that no man can find out the work that God maketh from the beginning to the end." (*Ecclesiastes* 3:11)

Just as nature always rebounds from its winters and draughts, Hamilton College president Melancthon Woolsey Stryker (1892–1917) wrote, so every emotional low holds out the promise of an eventual flourishing. "The harvests need the night as well as the day to ripen them," he would say. "It takes the whole quartet of the seasons to utter the fugal year."[239]

When DePauw University's Francis John McConnell (1909–1912) felt dissatisfied with his own life, he took comfort in imagining what it would have been like for a human observer to witness the creation as described in the first chapters of *Genesis*. For although God expressed satisfaction with each stage He completed, a mere mortal might easily miss the achievements. The light came, but it shone upon chaos. And while the division of the Earth's waters brought forth a multiplicity of species, to what point? Remembering our vision is limited, McConnell taught his students, helps us endure life's less pleasant transitions without succumbing to either escapist fantasy or religious cynicism.[240]

Help Yourself by Helping Others

The presidents also knew periods of moodiness and discontent are best tolerated by taking time to help someone whose unhappiness is even greater than one's own. A student with learning disabilities struggling to read, a handicapped neighbor unable to cook for himself, a friend or relative who has fallen on hard times—the exact service is less important than the willingness to lose oneself for a time in caring for another.

The effect may only be subtle at first, so subtle it can hardly be described. And yet it is not long before the giver discovers his or her life is not nearly as unsatisfying as it seemed. A "joy slips silently into our hearts," as Brown University president Ezekiel Gilman Robinson (1872–1889) once described the transformation, "and begins its melody there [even] before we are aware of its presence."[241]

University of Wisconsin president John Bascom (1874–1887) called giving of one's time to help others the closest thing to a genuine spiritual elixir, something with effects far more profound than simply being able to congratulate oneself for doing a good deed. Anytime we try to restore some part of the world to "what it ought to be," as he put it, "the mind of God opens upon us."[242] And in such moments, our moodiness and discontent inevitably recede.

Other early college presidents pointed to the famous passage in *Matthew*, where Jesus is asked by the lawyer which is the greatest commandment. That one should love God "with all thy heart, and with all thy soul, and with all thy mind," he replied. And then he quickly added a second commandment "like unto it," one should "love thy neighbor as thyself." On these two commandments, Jesus said, "hang all the law and the prophets." (*Matthew* 22:35–40)

In other words, we engage most intimately with God when we *labor by His side* to serve those in physical or emotional distress. And it is through such service we are infused with a genuine sense of accomplishment.

Modern psychologists have a truly inadequate phrase to describe the emotional benefits of caregiving, which they call the "empathy-altruism hypothesis."[243] But at least today's mental health professionals recognize something about helping others palliates moodiness and discontent. Indeed, the positive feelings accompanying charitable activity have been well-documented in many studies.[244]

Certainly, the millions of Americans who daily volunteer to nurse indigent patients, counsel immigrants, provide meals to the home-bound, conduct prison visitations, support homeless shelters, help those afflicted with HIV/AIDS, tutor students in distressed urban areas, or supervise programs to combat sexual trafficking would readily testify to the truth of the familiar saying: "When His good pleasure becomes your good pleasure, when your effort harmonizes entirely with His, then you will be happy."[245]

The Benedict Option

As we close our discussion of moodiness and discontent, I cannot ignore the growing number of today's Christians who would say this subject cannot be adequately addressed without recognizing the existence of an oppressively secular culture. It is not that they would disagree with the presidents' advice on how to handle the normal ebb and flow of spiritual inspiration, but many would say the periodic dissatisfaction they experience is compounded by something more sinister.

Comparing their plight to that of America's Puritan colonists who could no longer suffer the religious intolerance of

European society, they see themselves as victims of an increasingly oppressive materialism. In the words of Rod Dreher, senior editor of *The American Conservative*, today's Christians are effectively "living as exiles in their own country."[246]

Dreher has become a popular champion for what he calls the "Benedict Option," a modern variation on the example of Saint Benedict of Nursia, who laid the groundwork for the rebirth of Christianity as ancient Rome declined. To serve God's peace in today's world, Dreher argues, the true believer must withdraw as much as practically possible from conventional society and focus on explicitly Christian activities such as religiously-based homeschooling, the shared reading of spiritual classics, using faith-based alternatives to government programs, and even self-sufficient farming—all the while minimizing one's exposure to the mass media.[247]

If surveys are any indication, the number of Christians who agree with Dreher appears to be growing. A poll in the fall of 2015 by YouGov.com found a remarkable 53 percent of religious Americans now think they should forgo serving on local school boards, joining non-religious civic groups, or engaging in any kind of public service and instead devote themselves to a more spiritually robust subculture.[248]

That many Christians would feel this way is understandable. And there is certainly nothing wrong with pursuing any of the time-honored remedies Dreher advocates, if doing so is what one is called to do.

Yet it must also be said, no matter how far one thinks our present society has strayed from its religious roots, thoughtful believers have always been under attack for trying to live spiritually in the material world—if not by a secular culture, then by a superficially religious one. As Yale College president Noah Porter (1871–1886) warned in his final chapel address to the graduating class of 1873, "You go into a world in which atheistic theories are accepted with scarce a thought of their import, and anti-Christian suggestions are adopted on a half-hour's reading of a brilliant essay. While the world is in this condition, your faith in the Son of God may often be tried. It must be intelligent and thoughtful if it is to be zealous and strong."[249]

. My own view on the subject has been influenced for many years by an event that took place just after a talk I gave on "Spiritual Values and Emotional Health" to a group of engineers at the Minneapolis-based Medtronic Corporation. At the end of the question-and-answer session following my lecture, the person who invited me to speak asked if I would be interested in "seeing the heart of the company."

Since Medtronic was widely known as one of the great medical technology companies, I happily agreed and was soon being led out the door of the auditorium where I spoke and across a large plaza toward a tall office complex. I followed my host into the lobby of the building, where I saw on one side what looked like the employee cafeteria.

We turned in the opposite direction, and he led me through a door into a silent, beautifully-lit chamber. It was walled with shelves holding ornately decorated Bibles and other sacred artifacts from around the world, and in the center of the room, there was a comfortably carpeted meditation area.

My host explained I was in the Hermundslie Room, built with revenues from the company's first successful products and dedicated by Chairman Earl Bakken to the memory of his deceased brother-in-law, Palmer Hermundslie. I also learned that room was designed as a place where employees of every faith could come to seek "deeper guidance" for their personal and professional problems anytime of the day or night.

In the years since my visit to Medtronic, I am still struck by the extent of the unseen religious activity in American life, even in places where it has supposedly disappeared or been restricted. In 2011, while researching an article on how church groups were responding to the nationwide real estate collapse and subsequent financial crisis, I learned Protestant and Catholic organizations stepped up to become the largest providers of afterschool tutoring and homework programs for K-12 children everywhere in the country. Many churches spontaneously adopted run-down public schools, expanding their libraries, fixing their gyms, and even putting down carpeting—all done with sufficient discretion to not embarrass nervous superintendents with accusations of having unconstitutionally yielded to religious influences.

I have also been impressed over the years by how quickly the seeming strength of secular culture collapses in the face of genuine adversity. Research published in the *New England Journal of Medicine* just after the 9/11 attacks on New York City and Washington, DC, found an astonishing 90 percent of Americans coped with their stress, not by taking tranquilizers or reading some self-help guru or listening to cable news commentators, but by "turning to God." During the week following the terrorist assault, 60 percent went to a church or memorial service, and sales of the Bible rose more than 25 percent. Even before 2000, more than sixty published studies showed high rates of spiritual coping in people with medical problems ranging from arthritis to cancer.[250]

My point is simple: while secular influences are indeed both widespread and formidable, they are not nearly as deep as it so often seems. In the end, people still get promoted to positions of responsibility, not based on their looks, possessions, taste in fine wines, or even Ivy League educations, but because they incarnate the traditional Judeo-Christian virtues of honesty, dependability, humility, and respect for human rights. Similarly, those who are relied upon in times of crisis are not the sensually indulgent but the sensitive and disciplined. No one who serves God is truly handicapped—on the contrary, they often find doors opening exactly where or when the materialist would least expect it.

All this is not to underestimate the dangers of cultural materialism, especially where children are concerned. But as Scripture has always tried to remind us, real freedom comes not from trying to avoid the material world but having the wisdom to negotiate it. "That goodness which would thrive by getting into a little room and fastening all windows and doors will suffocate," Hamilton's Stryker once told his students. The Christian "will be forced constantly to his base of supplies, but he can be in the largest sense a man of affairs. He will, if he is a good soldier, be more anxious about the ammunition wagon than the ambulance."[251]

Reflection:

Peace I leave with you, my peace I give unto you:
not as the world giveth, give I unto you. Let not your
heart be troubled, neither let it be afraid.
—John *14:27*

LESSON TEN:

BE NOT INTIMIDATED BY THE WORLD OF COMMERCE

[The] study and practice of true piety is no hindrance to the vigorous prosecution of our secular pursuits; but, on the contrary, is favorable to our success in all our lawful undertakings. No mind can be in so favorable a state for attention to the ordinary studies or business of life as when it is conscious of being at peace with God, and of doing all things from a desire to serve and please Him.

—John Maclean Jr., president of Princeton College (1854 –1868)[252]

Now the great truth which the Savior…asserts is that a man's secular concerns are to be managed on precisely the same principles, and with reference to the same great ends, as his more directly religious engagements. There is not one set of rules for the

*acquisition and management of property and the
regulation of trade, and another for the regulation
of the heart, the business of religion, and the
preparation of the soul for the eternity before it. The
concerns of secular life are not to be placed in one
category, and those of religion in another, so that a
man may follow the corrupt maxims of trade and
stand well among tradesmen as a man of business,
and follow the law of Christ in connection with
the church and religion, and so stand well among
Christians as a pious man.*

—Samuel W. Fisher, president of
Hamilton College (1858–1866)[253]

*He who can assume to himself so much importance,
as to see no connection between his own prosperity
and the approbation of the wise and virtuous,
exhibits the most striking evidence that he is
travelling in the broad road of destruction.*

—Jonathan Maxcy, president of
Brown University (1792–1802)[254]

"There is a Place for You."

For a country settled by so many persecuted religious minorities, each initially inclined to be as self-protective and self-sufficient as possible, developing the spiritual wisdom to express one's calling in the wider world of commerce was, from the presidents' perspective, America's great cultural achievement. After all, if it were possible to be a good Christian in the one sphere of life where its maxims often seemed to have the least sway, then it could honestly be said faith had the power to triumph always and everywhere.

As early as the beginning of the nineteenth century, the Christian college presidents were already teaching courses in business and economics from a religious perspective. Francis Wayland, a one-time medical student whose abrupt conversion experience led to the pulpit of a Boston Baptist church and later to the presidency of Brown University (1826–1855), had an especially strong influence on undergraduates nationwide with two widely used textbooks, *The Elements of Moral Philosophy* and *The Elements of Political Economy*.

Much of what Wayland taught came from his own practical efforts to rescue Brown, which was nearly bankrupt when he arrived. In addition to the school's financial problems, its students were undisciplined, the faculty uninterested in campus life, and the curriculum had never been updated to include the latest advances in science and engineering.

As the school finally began to turn around, it seemed to Wayland the laws of economics and Christian teachings had much in common, in that both dealt with cause and effect. You do the right things in both business and faith, and you get a positive result. Conversely, you do the wrong things and failure is almost inevitable.[255]

From this, Wayland concluded the essence of worldly accomplishment lay in "applying the great religious maxims to everyday life."[256] He believed especially in the power of setting a moral example—of a leader not expecting from others what he or she does not require of oneself.[257] He was also impressed by the power of expressing one's honest opinion on every business matter, regardless of any imagined negative consequences.[258]

As the rules for commercial success and for serving God so closely overlap, he taught, it should come as no surprise that any career path born of holding the greatest thought, praying daily for God's guidance, and living within the bounds of His moral law will produce tangible evidence of Divine approval. There are places at the top of every profession for those who are spiritually prepared for them, he said. Or there will be, when they resolve to become fit.

Such was Wayland's influence that, by the early twentieth century, it was common for college presidents to study the lives of successful entrepreneurs and identify the spiritual values which led to their achievements. In his popular book *The Gospel of Good Will*, Bowdoin College president William DeWitt Hyde (1885–1917) devoted an entire chapter to the example of Long Island Railroad executive William H. Baldwin Jr., whose entire career was based on his belief the best business decisions are the most Christian ones.[259] In deciding whether and how to build a new rail line, for example, Baldwin was known for taking pains to ensure the interests of every imaginable party—not just customers and investors, but track layers, train operators, and residents of impacted communities—were taken into account.

Baldwin, an early trustee of Tuskegee Institute in 1894 and a strong supporter of its president, Booker T. Washington (1881–1915), also believed charitable activity was good for business, even when money was given to controversial groups. He was instrumental in raising sizable donations to educate African Americans from other businessmen and gave generously of his own money to help the families of former slaves.

Closer to our own time, it's been shown that the desire to express one's moral and spiritual values through work does, indeed, elevate an employee's contribution, no matter what his or her position in the organization. In 2001, for example, New York University researcher Amy Wrzesniewski and Jane Dutton from the University of Michigan became intrigued with the fact that some janitors at a large hospital worked much more diligently than others, so they reviewed in-depth interviews with twenty-eight cleaning staffers to find out why.

It soon became clear the productivity gap had nothing to do with salary, benefits, or how each got along with their supervisor, but how the employees defined their jobs. The more productive janitors saw their work, not as just a way to make a living, but as an opportunity to contribute to the hospital's healing process. Believing the way they picked up the trash, changed bed pans, or mopped around a patient's room had an impact on his or her recovery, they did it with greater care and thoroughness. "The contrasts among the cleaners were striking," said Wrzesniewski and Dutton ranging, "from how they described the skill level of the work to the kinds of tasks they would do."[260]

Going on to review a wider range of jobs—from hairdresser and kitchen helper to engineer and computer technician—

researchers Wrzesniewski and Dutton found a similar pattern. Those who contribute the most to a business or organization define their jobs, at least in their own minds, as an expression of lofty and deeply held values.

Wanting to further understand this connection between conviction and productivity, two Harvard professors, Rachel M. McCleary and Robert J. Barro, collected information on religious worship in nearly one hundred countries and related it to statistics on local development. They were struck by what turned out to be a very strong relationship between belief in an afterlife—especially in the exitance of both Heaven and Hell— and a region's economic progress.[261]

Of course, none of what the early college presidents first taught about religion and prosperity was ever intended to promote money-making for its own sake or to suggest every Christian is called to a financially rewarding career. Nor did the presidents claim every business venture undertaken in the Lord's name would prove profitable, at least in the commercial sense. The important thing, they believed, was to seek God's guidance and follow wherever it led, including to a business or profession. In other words, not to automatically assume a worldly calling is somehow spiritually inferior.

"I believe most solemnly that the great need of our times is the utter abolishment in Christian thinking [of the] high and mighty wall which we have built along the whole frontier of our everyday life, separating it from our religious life," Emory College president Atticus Greene Haygood (1876–1884) would tell his graduating seniors. "…there is absolutely no distinction in the essential nature of God's claim upon us or in the spirit of reverence and fidelity in which our service is to be rendered."[262]

"Skyhooks"

The great irony of our own very skeptical era is the extent to which modern management science has validated the spiritual prescriptions of the early college presidents. Despite the enduring market for self-help books with provocative titles like: *Winning Through Intimidation, The Leadership Secrets of Attila the Hun, Confessions of an S.O.B.*, and *Swim with the Sharks without Being Eaten Alive*, studies of actual business practices have for decades recommended a far more elevated approach to work.

One study undertaken in the early 1950s by Oliver Arthur Ohmann, then head of the Psychology Department at the Cleveland campus of Case Western Reserve University, is still widely taught in business schools across America. Wanting to learn more about how successful executives become that way, Ohmann took a temporary leave from his university position and landed a job as assistant to the President of the Standard Oil Company. Once hired, he initiated a series of in-depth interviews with top managers from both inside his firm and other large companies in the Cleveland area.

In 1955, Ohmann summarized his conversations in an article called "Skyhooks," which was quickly accepted by the *Harvard Business Review*. Featured soon after in a *Time* magazine story, the piece found an unusually large audience for an academic paper and was widely praised for its insights by high-level managers in businesses, non-profit organizations, and government agencies around the country.

Conceding at the very beginning of his article that any good executive must have some organizational ability and at least a basic understanding of standard accounting principles, Ohmann went on to argue that the skills taught in most business school textbooks were, at best, of secondary importance and completely missed the moral and spiritual basis of effective leadership. The most common trait of the successful leaders he interviewed was not the mastery of some management technique, but a philosophical outlook—"something deep inside that supports them." Not all were willing to use the word *God* or talk in detail about their religious convictions, but it was clear they were committed to "something ultimate, something personal, something beyond reason"[263] which had the practical effect of inspiring the trust and cooperation of other employees, even in constituencies normally antagonistic to management.

To illustrate this last point, Ohmann cited a story told him by Jacob D. Cox, one-time president of the Cleveland Twist Drill Company. Widely admired both for his business acumen and charitable activities, Cox had recently finished negotiating a new multi-year contract with his firm's workers, when he received an unscheduled visit from Jimmy Green, a union representative. Green wanted Cox to know that with almost every previous job, he went home feeling grouchy, never up to playing with his children or taking his wife out. "But since I have been working here all that has changed," Green admitted. "Now when I come home, the children run to meet me and we have a grand romp together. It is a wonderful difference and I don't know why, but I thought you would like to know."[264]

"Answered Prayers"

Because the presidents believed intuition to be central to living spiritually in the material world, it is interesting to note how many well-known businesspeople in our own time have attributed their success to following their "inner voice," regardless of what might seem more logical or prudent. "Trust your gut instinct over spreadsheets," as entrepreneur Naveen Jain, founder of InfoSpace and the space rocket company Moon Express, once put it. "There are too many variables in the real world that you simply can't put into a spreadsheet. Spreadsheets spit out results from your inexact assumptions and give you a false sense of security. In most cases, your heart and gut are still your best guide."[265]

Even today, people who check into a Hilton hotel will find a copy of the autobiography of founder Conrad Hilton, in which he confesses his lifelong interest in religion and his view of intuition as "answered prayer." You do the best you can to make the right decision—thinking, figuring, and planning; then you pray and wait to be called.

Whenever Hilton purchased an old building to make over into a hotel, it was never because of any hard-nosed calculation related to potential traffic or renovation expenses, but because he had literally "fallen in love" with the structure. He was never embarrassed to say his biggest projects always felt like the material expression of Divine guidance.

Oliver Ohmann came to appreciate the importance of intuition in his own life when some fifteen years after his landmark study for the *Harvard Business Review*, the magazine's editors asked him to write a retrospective commentary on how he came to write it. He agreed, but soon found it difficult to organize his ideas.

"After much reading and thinking, I got absolutely nowhere," Ohmann recalled. In desperation, he even considered abandoning the editor's request, but first decided to turn his stalled effort over to God. "Deep inside my consciousness I said, in effect, to my silent partner within, 'Look, if you want me to do this, you better help.' About 2 a.m. that morning the ideas flowed in a continuous stream, and I put them down in shorthand notes as fast as I could."[266]

A more scientific analysis of intuitive decision-making occurred in 1984, when Harvard Professor Daniel Isenberg announced the results of a major research project. For more than two years, he managed to persuade some of America's most respected executives to let him monitor their daily activities so he could get an idea of how they made their judgments.

"I conducted intensive interviews," he explained, "observed them on the job, read documents, talked with their colleagues and, in some cases, subordinates, and engaged them in various exercises in which they recounted their thoughts as they did their work." Altogether, Isenberg spent the equivalent of twenty-five days getting to know each manager on the job, even reading some of his observations out loud to get his subjects' reactions.

Far more important to successful decision-making than education, personality, or even organizational ability, Isenberg concluded, is the discipline to hold back on any final choice long enough for intuitive solutions to percolate into consciousness. Although "ambiguity can be destroying, [it can also] be very helpful to an operation," as one of Isenberg's managers had confided. Ambiguities "yield a certain freedom you need as a chief executive officer not to be nailed down on everything.... The fact is we tie ourselves too much to linear plans, to clear time scales. I like to fuzz up time scales completely."

Indeed, the more Isenberg studied his managers, the more he found they relied on intuition in all phases of business: They trust their intuitive sense that an unseen difficulty might exist, create full pictures of situations by combining partial information with personal experience, use intuition as a check on rational analysis, and depend on intuition to quickly bypass a more lengthy logical analysis of problems.

Isenberg's subjects did not completely forsake logic; in many cases, they used it to sharpen their intuitions and explain them to colleagues. But they prevented their desire for quick and logical answers from overriding the deeper wisdom of a good hunch.[267]

Apple Computer's famed co-founder Steve Jobs was not a Christian, but his commencement speech in praise of intuition to Stanford University's 2005 graduating class could well have been given by any of America's Christian college presidents. "Your time is limited," Jobs told the departing seniors. "Don't waste it living someone else's life. Don't be trapped by dogma, which is living the result of other people's thinking. Don't let the noise of others' opinions drown your own inner voice. Everything else is secondary."[268]

Moral Dilemmas as Spiritual Opportunities

We could, if we wished, look at each of the presidents' other principles for living spiritually in a secular world and show their compatibility with a successful business career. Yet I doubt any reader who has come this far needs any more convincing of at least a general connection between living well and doing well.

Neither, I would guess, is any reader seriously worried that wearing a crucifix, a "What-Would-Jesus-Do?" bracelet, or some other Christian symbol is going to hurt one's career prospects. As journalist Susan Pinker reported in her 2016 *Wall Street Journal* article on public displays of religious conviction, even atheists and agnostics tend to interpret them as marks of trustworthiness. "When we display our piety," Pinker concluded, "our social stock rises."[269]

The subject which does require our attention—as it will repeatedly challenge us throughout life—is how to deal with those thorny situations where the imagined consequences of doing the right thing seem excessively risky, while a seemingly small or undetectable moral compromise appears to offer us a way out. Like the problem of sexual harassment in the workplace which, as I write these words, is very much in the news. So many of the cases we hear about involve victims who felt it was safer to keep quiet about inappropriate but manageable advances by superiors rather than risk losing a job.

Or consider the case of the corporate executive who has discovered his firm has inadvertently put out a defective product and now feels pressured to disguise the fact, lest the company be subject to unfavorable publicity and even lawsuits. "Perhaps there is no need to admit the real problem," the person is tempted to think. "After all, most of the faulty items can still be recalled unsold from stores. Any consumer who has purchased one is unlikely to be seriously harmed and, if he or she finds the product deficient, will simply want to return or exchange it."

Former Johnson & Johnson chairman James Burke once faced an even more serious dilemma than this, and his determination to find a moral resolution is still discussed in business school classes around the world.[270] It was September of 1982 when Burke first learned one of the pharmaceutical company's most profitable products had been maliciously sabotaged, killing seven people. Someone whose identity is still a mystery apparently penetrated the packaging for several bottles of the non-prescription painkiller Tylenol, replacing the original capsules with cyanide-laced lookalikes that killed seven people in the Chicago area.

There were several things Burke could have done to limit the financial and reputational damage to his company. He could have issued a recall for every box of Tylenol on Chicago store shelves, for example. He also could have offered a generous reward for information leading to the culprit's arrest. Or run an ad campaign designed to assure the rest of the country the poisonings were localized.

But then Burke asked himself an essentially spiritual question: What was the maximum he could do to absolutely guarantee customers' safety from even the most improbable consequence of the Tylenol meddling?

That fall, at a cost of $100 million, Johnson & Johnson recalled and destroyed every package of its flagship painkiller, made announcements warning people to hold off buying the product until it could create a new kind of tamper-proof bottle, and completely reorganized the company's manufacturing facilities. Together, these actions constituted a financial setback some thought would cost Burke his job. But he was willing to gamble he could sustain the public's trust in Tylenol over the long run if he were to go as far as he could to guarantee product safety in the short run.

Which is exactly what happened. A year later, Johnson & Johnson's share of the $1.2 billion analgesic market had climbed back almost to where it was before the poisonings.

One of the great contributions of the early college presidents to their own time was to identify the temptation to make a seemingly convenient moral compromise as a special kind of dilemma, one with the potential to yield unexpected blessings if tackled courageously. It is the kind of opportunity symbolized for centuries by the *Old Testament* story of Joseph, whose willingness to choose what was right over what was safe—even at the cost of being sold into slavery at one time and being thrown into prison at another—enabled him to become Pharaoh's chief advisor and one of the most respected men in ancient Egypt.

Of course, the presidents were realistic enough to know, being human, we all face situations where our faith will not be up to the spiritual opportunity. Even the apostle Peter was reduced to denying Christ on the day of the crucifixion, not just once but three times.

But what the presidents also knew is we all have some capacity to struggle at the margins. And taking time to think through different ways of handling a delicate or embarrassing situation—

talking it over with a spouse, close friend, or trusted advisor—always extends the initially assumed limits of our moral courage.

Most importantly, we have, through prayer, unlimited access to the wisest problem solver in the universe. "If any of you lack wisdom, let him ask of God, that giveth to all *men* liberally, and upbraideth not; and it shall be given him." (*James* 1:5)

Our secular culture admittedly makes it feel odd to ask for God's help, even moral help, around a practical business matter, but that's just another example of the soft atheism we discussed in Lesson Four—what Scripture calls "double-minded" thinking (*James* 1:8). In other words, we haven't yet resolved to serve the Lord in every sphere of life. Asking for His guidance on a thorny work issue is not prevailing too much or inappropriately but only catching up to where we should be.

Some years ago, I knew the executive director of a charity who was having a problem with the chairman of the group's board. This man was constantly pressing the executive director to pay his expenses to conventions of like-minded charities, even though that would not have been the best use of scarce funds and, therefore, a betrayal of the group's donors. The executive director resisted the pressure but suspected the chairman was spitefully sabotaging his reputation with the other board members.

Fortunately, the executive director had developed a practice of seeking daily guidance each morning from his Real Chair and eventually had an inspiration: to imagine himself in the mind of the person pestering him for travel expenses—and to do so with the idea of trying to identify something good in what the man was seeking. "What if he really wants to be more involved in our work," the executive director thought, "and going to conventions is just the easiest way for him to do it?"

From then on, my acquaintance made a practice of frequently updating the chairman between formal board meetings and even asking him to take on some operating responsibilities. What had really been going on in the chairman's mind will likely remain a mystery, but his inappropriate travel expense requests stopped.

"Don't Say What You Don't Think"

When it comes to business ethics, said Union College president Eliphalet Nott (1804–1866), the least we should expect of ourselves is to avoid advocating positions we privately oppose, just to fit in with the crowd or avoid controversy. We may not always have the courage to fully express what we believe to be right, but the simple determination not to contradict ourselves, however subtly we manage it, can often prove a great spiritual accomplishment. It was a lesson Nott learned early in his career, when serving as pastor of the Presbyterian church in Albany, New York.

The year was 1804, and Alexander Hamilton had just died from wounds after his famous duel with Aaron Burr. Nott knew his congregation would expect a sermon on the incident but found himself torn. On the one hand, the clergyman was aware his distaste for the popular custom of resolving grievances in a shootout was controversial and expressing disapproval would almost certainly provoke an angry backlash. Yet the circumstances of Hamilton's unexpected death could not be ignored.

Eulogizing the Revolutionary War hero and statesman without mentioning how he died would falsely imply Nott's approval of the practice.

Moved by the plight of Hamilton's family—and knowing even those who supported dueling could not deny its emotional cost—Nott decided to focus his sermon on the suffering of anyone who has ever lost a close relative or friend to a duel. It was not the most direct argument against what he believed to be a barbaric carryover from medieval Europe, but at least it kept him from appearing to condone it.

Nott's sermon was still criticized, although not nearly as much as he feared. His unexpected satisfaction came from learning of the many Americans in other states who, inspired by transcripts of his comments, developed their own arguments against dueling. Indeed, because he found a way to tactfully express his disapproval, legislatures across the country came under increasing pressure to ban the practice. Back in New York, the trustees of Union College in Schenectady were so impressed with Nott's sermon they invited him to become the school's president, a position he held for an astonishing sixty-two years.[271]

Perhaps the most impressive example of Nott's refusal to give false ascent in our own time involves the Russian novelist Aleksandr Solzhenitsyn in the years before the fall of the Berlin Wall. To those Eastern European dissidents who no longer believed in their governments' communist ideology but were understandably afraid to be too critical, his advice was simply, "don't say what you don't think."

Would-be rebels did not have to go "around preaching the truth at the top of [their] voice," Solzhenitsyn said. Neither did they have to take up arms or risk starting an underground press. Such is the power of collectively refusing to endorse what you do not believe, he promised them, it would eventually cause their corrupt regimes to fall—which the tyrannical satellite governments of the old Soviet Union finally did.[272]

A series of events involving my own daughter provide a far less dramatic example of what happens in the wake of refusing to contradict one's beliefs, but an instructive one nonetheless. The lesson goes back to her freshman year at a college in Scotland. Compared to her classmates, her political views were very conservative—a fact she never paraded, but neither would she feign more liberal convictions just to fit in.

One result was she was asked by a group of American Republicans living in Europe to be a college representative to their group. Again, this was not because she was politically outspoken. It was that there were so few US students at British schools who identified themselves as conservative, the Republicans were just happy to find one.

Years later, my daughter had a job as the media representative for an economics think tank in London, a position that required her to work with local radio and television news producers. Her on-air appearances were relatively few until early 2016, when the British public became fascinated with Donald Trump's run for office. Realizing somebody they knew was once an official member of the overseas Republican group, her media contacts started putting her on camera almost every day to comment on the ups and downs of the White House contest.

Today, my daughter is a frequent broadcast commentator and columnist in the United Kingdom, an unusual accomplishment for any American, let alone someone so young. Clearly her success is the result of many factors, but it would never have happened if, years before, she was tempted to say what she did not think, just to fit in at school.

"This is my effort and my contribution."

There is a reason, the early college presidents knew, why people in every age have a fondness for the odysseys of heroes or heroines who struggle to retain their integrity against difficult odds, only to triumph in the end. Whether it is Virgil's *Aeneid*, *Don Quixote*, any of Dickens' novels, or the contemporary *Lord of the Rings* trilogy, such tales illustrate a spiritual law too diffused in its unfolding ever to be precisely documented, but valid nonetheless.

Nor is it a coincidence the central figure in such stories typically joins up with an admirable traveling companion not long before his or her character is about to be severely tested. Nothing so quickly reveals the way around a seemingly insurmountable barrier than the advice and support of another idealist.

Reflecting on the fact his undergraduates would soon enter a world where "a thousand excuses and extenuations in favor of covert dishonesty...will press upon you day by day," Hamilton College president Samuel W. Fisher (1858–1866) nevertheless assured them "if you are faithful to the great principles of Christian morals in the beginning, the path of rectitude will grow firm and straight beneath your feet, and upon you will fall the benedictions of your fellow men; while within you a conscience void of offense to man will ever sing of peace and hope."

"There is that in mercantile integrity, even when it is divorced from Christian principle," Fisher noted, "which brings with it a reward to its possessor and commands for him the respect of men. But there is in Christian integrity, in the morality, which springs from the love of God and men, a vastly nobler benediction, which as a fountain of peace never ceases to flow. It is in the heart a perpetual spring, of purity and joy, blessing the possessor, and blessing the world."[273]

Some years back, on one of my occasional trips to visit my mother's side of the family in Davenport, Iowa, I met Joe Kimmel, a family friend who gave me a copy of a manuscript written by his father in the late 1940s. The elder Kimmel was a successful businessman in the Midwest, starting as a young salesman with the old National Cash Register Company, then working as an executive for a division of General Motors, and, after several failed attempts to start his own business, finally founded what became a thriving electrical supply company.

Throughout the ups and downs of his career, Kimmel was sustained by his belief that whatever success he enjoyed came, not from any management skill, but from staying true to his family's religious values, what he termed "learning to get along with yourself." He began each morning with a simple affirmation: "This day I will consciously treat everyone with kindness and consideration. I will not take offense. I will do what I can to add to the good will in the world. This is my effort and my contribution."

Toward the end of his life, the elder Kimmel could justifiably point to many accomplishments, both in business and as an active member of Davenport's many civic groups. Yet he measured his own success, neither by the number of his possessions nor even the esteem in which he was held by the community, but by his relationship with God.

"Even as physical laws govern the whirling spheres in their orbits," he wrote in language easily mistaken for a sermon by an eloquent old-time college president, so higher "laws govern the lives of individuals on this planet.... The system of the planets, the growth of the trees, the wonderful qualities of the human body and mind...[the beauty of this] great Kingdom is open to all...conditioned only that the aspirant be clothed in the qualities of the spirit."[274]

There have been—are—and always will be people like Joe Kimmel's father, people whose prosperity and prestige in the community validate the courage to live spiritually in the material world. They may never get the same attention as practitioners of the latest management fad, but they are the real American success story.

Reflection:

And let us not be weary in well doing: for in due season we shall reap, if we faint not.
—Galatians *6:9*

THE SPIRITUAL EXPERIENCE OF THE MATERIAL WORLD

That subtle sense of the beautiful and the sublime which accompanies spiritual insight, and is part of it—this is the highest achievement of which humanity is capable.

—Nicholas Murray Butler, president of Columbia University (1902–1945)[275]

What better path can be thrown up for us, with more bracing air and commanding outlook than this which treads along the narrow ridge between the purely natural and the purely supernatural, between Nature and God, Earth and Heaven, disclosing the forces to be met and worked with there, disclosing the light, the promises, the powers that flow in upon us here, ready for a spiritual, a truly potent, ministration in our behalf? He who lifts and pries in the physical world alone...may not appreciate this.

—John Bascom, president of the University of Wisconsin (1874–1887)[276]

Now in these happy peaceful days, with the world before us, is the time to begin to live in this true sense. Do not be afraid of being alone, of facing your own problems without external aid; for if we truly seek the Lord, He shall be found, and we shall begin truly to live.

—Caroline Hazard, president of Wellesley College (1899–1910)[277]

Special Effects Spirituality

It is a measure of the extent to which so many moderns have lost touch with the wisdom of the early college presidents that the popular notion of a spiritual experience has come to imply a spectacular vision or overwhelming emotion, the theological equivalent of a big screen special effect. How many people when they hear the phrase think of Charlton Heston's Moses blinded by the burning bush or some dazzling display for an *Indiana Jones* movie?

By the late 1960s, the concept of spirituality had already become so disconnected from everyday life many otherwise intelligent people thought it could only be known by retreating to a mountaintop cave, going into group therapy, floating blindfolded in a sensory deprivation tank, or meditating under the influence of a Tibetan guru. Many even tried to bootstrap "higher consciousness" with mescaline, LSD, and other mind-altering drugs, a dangerous recourse which unfortunately persists to this day.

It is certainly true the spontaneous conversion of religious skeptics is often accompanied by what they describe as a "mental earthquake"—most famously St. Paul on the road to Damascus and the Christian philosopher Augustine of Hippo in a Milanese garden. After years of researching the history of such accounts for his 1902 classic, *The Varieties of Religious Experience*, Harvard professor William James found many conversion experiences are punctuated by an unforgettable flash of white light. (That is why it remains customary to say a person who has been enlightened on some subject has "seen the light.")

It is also possible for those who already believe to have an unusually penetrating experience of the kind famously described in a 1916 issue of the *Atlantic Monthly*. Initially reported anonymously by a woman later revealed to be Margaret Prescott Montague, it occurred at a surgical hospital where she was recuperating from a previous day's operation. No sooner had her bed been wheeled outside her room and onto the hospital gallery, when all the life around her began to radiate what she called an "unspeakable joy, beauty, and importance."[278]

As Montague recounted the experience, it was as if she were seeing her familiar world with "all the usual things" but more intensely—each man, woman, animal, and even flower and tree irresistibly riveting. "Every human being moving across that [hospital] porch," she wrote, "every sparrow that flew, every branch tossing in the wind, was caught in and was part of the whole mad ecstasy of loveliness...."[279] The entire event, which she later guessed lasted around twenty minutes, left her feeling Heaven "is here and now, before our very eyes, surging up to our very feet, lapping against our hearts, but we alas know not how to let it in!"[280]

What unexpectedly turned out to be widespread praise for Montague's account would suggest such ecstatic interludes are more common than generally realized. One reader responded, "I am a very ordinary woman, living a very ordinary life, my days... given up to housework—tending my furnace, cooking, dusting, washing dishes; but somehow these duties are never really gray. In the heart of them there is a glow."[281] Another said Montague's article expressed the world's beauty as she "felt it all my life."[282] And still another: "It seems to me that [such experiences are] not by accident" and never "leave us."[283]

So strongly did many identify with Montague's experience that a year later, in 1917, a New York publisher issued a book called *Twenty Minutes of Reality*, which included her original *Atlantic* essay along with a collection of readers' responses. It was eventually condensed into an article for the *Reader's Digest* and has since been reprinted many times over.

But while the state Montague described is by no means rare, neither is it universal, even among the most devoted Christians. And even if it were possible to somehow create circumstances which make it more likely to undergo something like it, it is not clear most people should—or would even want to—try. We know from James's research that dramatic spiritual awakenings are most often proceeded by a period of intense suffering:

on the heels of some humiliating failure, at the bottom of an alcohol or drug addiction, while serving time in prison, after a long struggle with a guilty conscience, or in the aftermath of a deadly tragedy. What Montague might have suffered prior to her remarkable awakening is not clear, but it did occur in a hospital after a major surgery.

Subtle Spirituality

On the other hand, there is a subtler, more enduring experience which comes to all who serve God through the material world—a shading of everyday events. And while certainly less overtly spectacular than a Hollywood special effect, it seems to make all the difference when it comes to the quality of a human life. It explains why a wealthy business owner can be miserable while one of his junior employees hums cheerfully through the day, or why a famous rock star wants to commit suicide while his high school music teacher finds contentment in the progress of a few talented students, or even why the world traveler can become world-weary while the cousin who rarely strays far from home sees something new in each day.

It is the difference reverberating in passages throughout Scripture: "But the path of the just *is* as the shining light, that shineth more and more unto the perfect day." (*Proverbs* 4:18) "…[H]e that hath clean hands shall be stronger and stronger." (*Job* 17:9) "But they that wait upon the Lord shall renew *their* strength; they shall mount up with wings as eagles; they shall run, and not be weary; *and* they shall walk, and not faint."

(*Isaiah* 40:31) "…[H]e being not a forgetful hearer, but a doer of the work, this man shall be blessed in his deed." (*James* 1:25)

If the presidents added anything to these time-honored promises, it was their observation that the joy of the spiritual mind is greatly enhanced by the daily habit of taking a few quiet moments to thank God for the good things that have happened to us over the previous twenty-four hours. Even if all we can seem to come up with on some especially tough days is a good meal, a pleasant conversation with a friend, or something interesting we've read, the repeated recall of everyday blessings has the cumulative effect of making us feel more grateful and optimistic than we would otherwise be.

"A devout temper," Brown University president Francis Wayland (1827–1855) explained to his students, is "cultivated by the exercise of devotion." The more consistently we express our gratitude to God for what daily life has given us, "the more profound, and pervading, and intense, and habitual will these feelings become."[284]

Today we know the physical and psychological effects of daily thanking God are so powerful they can be objectively demonstrated. Thankfulness is a "spiritual emotion," says David Rosmarin, director of the Spirituality and Mental Health Program at McLean Hospital and assistant professor at the Harvard Medical School, but a spiritual emotion at least partially quantifiable.

In one study, Dr. Rosmarin questioned 400 subjects to determine how grateful they felt toward life, to what extent their appreciation stemmed from a religious outlook, and their physical and emotional well-being. He was not surprised to discover all people who score high on gratitude have less anxiety than others, experience fewer depressions, and have a greater sense of well-being. But for those whose gratitude was expressed as an appreciation for what God gave them, these benefits were greatly magnified.[285]

In another study conducted by two prominent Christian scholars, Robert Emmons and Michael McCullough, subjects were divided into three groups. The first was told to keep a journal of the things they were grateful for each day. Those in the second group had to make a daily list of the various hassles they encountered. And a third control group simply described matter-of-factly what was happening in their lives, good or bad.

After ten weeks, those recording hassles and those objectively describing everyday events appeared about the same, but the gratitude group showed significant changes. It wasn't just that they were feeling predictably more optimistic about their lives, but they exercised more, slept better, felt more refreshed, and were even less often sick than the others.[286]

In addition to daily giving thanks for one's blessings, the presidents believed the spiritual sense could be greatly enhanced by frequent exposure to natural settings, where the artificial constructs and assumptions required to negotiate material reality can, for a time, be safely suspended—and the soul encouraged to identify with something beyond its body. The splendor of the night sky, the glory of the sunset, the serenity of the mountains, the magnificence of the ocean, the morning fog slowly lifting over a vast forest—the religiously-minded experience all such vistas with a luminescence carried over into the workaday world.

In this sense, the early college presidents were like the contemporary award-winning philosopher Charles Taylor, who says the power of modern secularism does not come from proving religion wrong, but from thickly papering it over with materialistic habits of thought.[287] One spiritual cure, therefore, is to periodically resume direct contact with the overwhelming wonders of God's creation.

"What is the purpose of natural beauty?" Randolph-Macon College president John A. Kern (1897–1899) would often ask his students. Is it a mere change of pace, or the opportunity to breathe fresher air? "There are those no doubt, who so regard it," he said. "But if there be the spiritual mind, the sense of the beautiful will have its own true revelation to make of an unseen glory."[288]

Milwaukee-Downer College co-founder Catharine E. Beecher (1850–1852) was especially poetic on the subject: "The heavings of the ocean, the rush of the tornado, the sheeted lightning, and the talking of fierce thunderbolts [become] expressions of His dignity and power," she wrote. "The whispers of evening, the low murmur of waters, the soft melodies of nature…are the breathings of His love. In the graceful movements of vegetable life, in gliding shadows and curling vapors, in the delicately blending colors, and in the soft harmonies of animated existence [we may discover] his gentleness, purity, and grace. The sighing of the wind, the moaning of the wood, the beaming of some lonely star, [and] the pensive gleam of moonlight recalls his tenderness and pitying sympathy."[289]

The scientists of our own time have yet to study how far nature amplifies the spiritual sense, but its well-documented ability to boost measures of vitality and optimism in general suggests the presidents were likely right. We know, for example, people who spend time in nature are less likely to obsess over problems or to entertain negative thoughts.[290]

In 2010, a British ecological economist named George MacKerron created an iPhone app called Mappiness, which periodically tracked some 20,000 volunteers to find out where they were, what they were doing, and how they were feeling at the time. Unsurprisingly, his subjects were least happy at work or while sick and most happy with friends and loved ones. But it also turned out, no matter what the experience, it was markedly improved by being outdoors, especially in non-urban settings. "Our nervous systems are built to resonate with…the natural world," writes Florence Williams, author of *The Nature Fix*. Science, she says, is bearing out what previous generations believed to be true.

The Comfort and Consolation

The early college presidents had many phrases for the more usual kind of spiritual experience I've been describing. Brown University's Jonathan Maxcy (1792–1802) called it "true happiness."[291] President Mary Lyon (1837–1849) of the Mt. Holyoke Female Seminary liked the expression "walking with Him."[292] Emory College president Atticus Greene Haygood (1876–1884) spoke of "the peace that is one's own,"[293] and for University of Chicago president William Rainey Harper (1891–1906), it was the "perfect peace of mind."[294]

But most often they spoke of the "comfort and consolation"[295] that comes from being focused on God's present will. Like the passenger at a bustling railroad station, where many train lines converge and thousands of people are rushing back and forth, the spiritual person at least has the confidence of knowing he or she is always on the right conveyance.

This focus on the present does not mean, as is sometimes said of the spiritual mind, it never dwells on the future. It is rather that any conclusions drawn are not automatically presumed to be an obligation of such speculation, nor are they allowed to undermine one's readiness to serve God in a completely different way, if called to do so.

Neither is the spiritual mind spared the stings of periodic stress, disappointment, or other painful emotions. Its blessing is not the absence of negative emotion but the realization that what we call "negative" and "positive" are often two inseparable aspects of the same thing. Anxiety, it turns out, is intimately related to excitement, just as loneliness is to the opportunity to grow closer to God, and even as depression is to the rebound from a misplaced trust or infatuation.

Milwaukee-Downer's Beecher never forgot how, as a young teacher at the Hartford Seminary in Connecticut, she periodically contemplated a serious study of the connection between Biblical precepts and mental health. But not until sickness forced her to take a leave of absence from work did she finally have the opportunity to do it. With little else to occupy her days, she first wrote a journal article on the subject and then a privately printed book, which was widely praised by many college presidents of her day. Looking back on the experience, Beecher had to admit, while she would never wish to be that sick again, she might never have written *The Elements of Mental and Moral Philosophy, Founded upon Experience, Reason and the Bible* without being involuntarily bedridden.[296]

Everyday spirituality does not even mean being free of the occasional temptation to do those things one knows are hurtful or self-destructive, for temptation alone is not always a bad development. As Antioch College president Horace Mann (1853–1859) would reassure the undergraduates who gathered weekly for his chapel sermons, the discipline required to check such impulses is proof we are free beings and our behavior is not helplessly determined by forces beyond our control. It is also a reminder, however poorly we may have acted in the past, we have become something better.

"The word *temptation* is never properly used in a good sense," Mann would say. It only implies the possibility of evil, a susceptibility, not evil itself. Christ "was tempted in all points, like as we are." Indeed, "one who is totally bad, who cannot be worse than he is, cannot be tempted. He has already…reached his nethermost. There is no more room for him to fall or grow downwards."[297]

The Quiet Delight

What a more common spirituality does mean is the serenity of believing the best one can do in life is to try to serve God at each moment. As William James put it, it "consists of the belief that there is an unseen order, and that our supreme good lies in harmoniously adjusting ourselves to it."[298]

Or as Bowdoin College president William DeWitt Hyde (1885–1917) liked to say, the growing conviction of what Jesus promised in his Sermon on the Mount—namely, putting what God wants first will incidentally get a person all the things he or she truly needs. This does not mean every earthly reward the believer once dreamt of achieving will come to pass. It does not mean having what the world regards as a powerful or prestigious title. And it certainly does not mean getting only those things which the body finds pleasurable.

But it does mean getting what one's soul—one's real, eternal self—fundamentally requires: the assurance that each moment offers the opportunity to live as one should. "I say unto you, Lift your eyes, and look on the fields; for they are white already to harvest." (*John* 4:35)

This high and precious consciousness "does not fall into the lap of the spiritually indolent," Hyde was quick to add. To get it, one must risk acting as if it were true, not just in the company of like-minded believers, but in the whole of one's life. To retain it, one must always be sensitive to God's call, regardless where it leads. And to increase it year by year, one must ennoble every encounter with the reminder other people are more than just background scenery or objects for our gratification. One must also never forget to take a few moments at the end of each day to give thanks for all the good things that have happened, be they what the world considers important events or just a good meal and a pleasant conversation.

Spiritual growth is a slow, sometimes uneven, and occasionally frustrating process, he conceded; "yet to those who seek God in these earnest practical social ways, this blessedness is as real as what we find in the most intimate human relationships. It comes to stay and it increases as the years go by."[299]

It is not always obvious a loving God exists and that a caring hand has framed and guides our world. His love takes such wide circuits, puts so many breaks on impulse and pleasure, and takes so much time to lay the foundations for any visible success that it is easy to conclude the opposite. But for the courageous believer, there will be moments in every day when he or she cannot help but be awed by the simple fact of one's own consciousness, the gift of Him who "filleth all in all." (*Ephesians* 1:23) The spiritual experience of the material world may not have the explosive color of a Hollywood special effect, but it is what the old-time college presidents meant when they spoke of a quiet delight in serving our ever-present Lord.

Reflection:

Peace I leave with you, my peace I give unto you:
not as the world giveth, give I unto you. Let not your
heart be troubled, neither let it be afraid.
—John *14:27*

BIBLIOGRAPHY

Andrews, L., "The Religious, Ambitious Lose Faith in America," *RealClearPolicy.com*. March 7, 2016.

Angell, J. B., *Honesty*. Ann Arbor, MI: University of Michigan, 1906.

Angell, J. B., *Knowledge and Wisdom*. Ann Arbor, MI: University of Michigan, 1904.

Barrows, John H., ed., *The World's Parliament of Religions: An Illustrated and Popular Story of the World's First Parliament of Religions, Held in Chicago in Connection with the Columbia Exposition of 1893*, Vols. I and II. Chicago: Parliament Publishing Company, 1893.

Bascom, J., *Evolution and Religion*. New York: G. P. Putnam's Sons, 1897.

Bascom, J., *The Science of Mind*. New York: G. P. Putnam's Sons, 1881.

Bascom, J., *Science, Philosophy and Religion*. New York: G. P. Putnam's Sons, 1871.

Bascom, J., *Sermons and Addresses*. New York: G. P. Putnam's Sons, 1913.

Bascom, J., *Things Learned by Living*. New York: G. P. Putnam's Sons, 1913.

Beecher, C. E., *Educational Reminiscences and Suggestions*. New York: J. B. Ford and Company, 1874.

Beecher, C. E., *The Elements of Mental and Moral Philosophy, Founded upon Experience, Reason and the Bible*. Hartford, CT: James B. Gleason, 1831.

Beecher, C. E., *Letters on the Difficulties of Religion*. Hartford, CT: Belknap and Hamersley, 1836.

Bennis, W. G., and Thomas, R. J., "Crucibles of Leadership," *On Mental Toughness*. Boston: Harvard Business School, 2018, pp. 9–24.

Bernstein, E., "The Surprising Boost You Get from Strangers," *Wall Street Journal*. May 11, 2019.

Berzoff, J., "Narratives of Grief and Their Potential for Transformation," *Palliative & Supportive Care*. Vol. 4, 2006, pp. 121–127.

Bonnefon, J.; Feeney, A.; and De Neys, W., "The Risk of Polite Misunderstandings," *Current Directions in Psychological Science*. Vol. 20, 2011, pp. 321–324.

Brody, J., "Positive Emotions May Extend Life," *New York Times*. March 28, 2017, p. D5.

Brooks, A., "Nice People Really Do Have More Fun," *Wall Street Journal*. October 19, 2016, p. A15.

Burtchaell, J. T., *The Dying of the Light*. Grand Rapids, MI: William B. Eerdmans, 1998.

Butler, N. M., *The Meaning of Education and Other Essays*. New York: Macmillan Company, 1905.

Butler, N. M., *Scholarship and Service*. New York: Charles Scribner's Sons, 1921.

Campbell, D. T., "On the Conflicts between Biological and Social Evolution and between Psychology and Moral Tradition," *American Psychologist.* Vol. 30, 1975, pp. 1103–1126.

Carter, F., *Mark Hopkins.* Boston: Houghton, Mifflin and Company, 1892.

Connley, C., "Suzy Welch: This Is the One Trait That Separates Successful People from Everyone Else," *www.cnbc.com.* January 29, 2019.

Conwell, R., and Shackleton, R., *Acres of Diamonds.* ReadaClassic. com, 2009.

Crooks, G., ed., *Sermons by Bishop Matthew Simpson.* New York: Harper and Brothers, 1885.

Darling, H., *Grief and Duty.* Albany, NY: S.R. Gray, 1865.

Davis, H., *Farewell Address to the Students of Hamilton College.* New York: J. and J. Harper, 1833.

Dempsey, E. F., ed., *Wit and Wisdom of Warren Akin Candler.* Nashville, TN: Cokesbury Press, 1922.

Disney, W., "There's Always a Solution," *Guideposts.* June, 1949, pp. 1+.

Dodge, E., *The Evidences of Christianity.* Boston: Gould and Lincoln, 1869.

Dowd, J., *Life of Braxton Craven.* Raleigh, NC: Edwards and Broughton, 1896 edition.

Dowd, J., *The Life of Braxton Craven.* Durham, NC: Duke University Press, 1939 edition.

Dreher, R., "Orthodox Christians Must Now Learn to Lives as Exiles in Our Own Country," *www.Time.com.* June 26, 2015.

Dubiel, R., *The Road to Fellowship.* Lincoln, NE: iUniverse, 2004.

Duffield, J., ed., *The Princeton Pulpit*. New York: Charles Scribner, 1852.

Duhigg, C., "Wealthy, Successful, and Miserable," *New York Times Magazine*. February 21, 2019.

Dunn, B. D., et al, "Listening to Your Heart: How Interoception Shapes Emotion Experience and Intuitive Decision Making," *Psychological Science*. Vol. 21, 2010, pp. 1835–1844.

Dwight IV, T., *Sermons*, Vols. I and II. New Haven, CT: Hezekiah Howe and Dukrie and Peck, 1828.

Dwight V, T., *Thoughts of and for the Inner Life*. New York: Dodd, Mead and Company, 1899.

Eastwood, J., Frischen, A., Fenske, M., and Smilek, D., "The Unengaged Mind: Defining Boredom in terms of Attention," *Perspectives on Psychological Science*. Vol. 7, pp. 482–495.

Entwistle, D., *Integrative Approaches to Psychology and Christianity*. Eugene, OR: Cascade Books, 2015.

Faber, J., and King, J., *How to Talk So Little Kids Will Listen*. New York: Scribner, 2017.

Fisher, S. W., *Sermon Occasioned by the Death of Miss Mary S. Dwight*. Albany, NY: Erastus H. Pease, 1845.

Fisher, S. W., *Three Great Temptations of Young Men*. Cincinnati: Moore, Wilstach, Keys and Company, 1860.

Fiske, F., ed., *Recollections of Mary Lyon*. Boston: American Tract Society, 1866.

Franklin, B., *The Autobiography of Benjamin Franklin*. Chicago: Lakeside Press, 1903.

Greene, M., *Fruitfulness on the Front Line*. Nottingham, England: Inter-Varsity Press, 2014.

Greene, M., *Thank God It's Monday*. Edinburgh: Muddy Pearl, 2019.

Hadley, A. T., *Baccalaureate Addresses*. New York: Charles Scribner's Sons, 1907.

Halsey, L., *A Sketch of the Life and Educational Labors of Philip Lindsley*. Hartford, CT: Williams, Wiley and Turner: reprinted from September 1859 issue of *Bernard's American Journal of Education*.

Halsey, L., ed., *Memoir of the Life and Character of Rev. Lewis W. Green*. New York, Charles Scribner, 1871.

Hanson, R., *Resilient*. New York: Harmony Books, 2018.

Harper, W. R., *Religion and the Higher Life: Talks to Students*. Chicago: University of Chicago Press, 1904.

Haygood, A. G., *Jack-Knife and Brambles*. Nashville, TN: Publishing House of the Methodist Episcopal Church, Barbee and Smith – Agents, 1893.

Haygood, A. G., *Sermons and Speeches*. Nashville, TN: Southern Methodist Publishing House, 1883.

Hazard, C., *The College Year*. Boston: Houghton, Mifflin and Company, 1910.

Hazard, C., *Prayers Offered in Wellesley College Chapel*. Printed privately for the Class of 1903, copy 11.

Herrera, T., "Let Go of Your Grudges. They're Doing You No Good." *New York Times*, May 19, 2019, p. B7.

Hopkins, M., Woodward, S., and Hoar, S., *Address to the People of Massachusetts on the Present Condition and Claims of the Temperance Reformation*. Boston: Massachusetts Temperance Union, 1846.

Hopkins, M., *Miscellaneous Essays and Discourses*. Boston: T. R. Marvin, 1847.

Hora, T., *Beyond the Dream*. Orange, CA: PAGL Press, 1986.

Hora, T., *Dialogues in Metapsychiatry*. New York: Seabury, 1977.

Hora, T., *Existential Metapsychiatry*. New York: Seabury, 1977.

Hyde, W. D., *Abba Father: or, the Religion of Everyday Life*. New York: Fleming H. Revell Company, 1908.

Hyde, W. D., *Are You Human?* New York: Macmillan Company, 1916.

Hyde, W. D., *Gospel of Good Will*. New York: Macmillan Company, 1916.

Hyde, W. D., *Jesus' Way*. Boston; Houghton: Mifflin and Company; 1903.

Hyde, W. D., *The Quest of the Best*. New York: Thomas Y. Crowell, 1913.

Hymowitz, K., "Is There Anything Grit Can't Do?" *Wall Street Journal*. June 24, 2017, p. A11.

Isenberg, D., "How Senior Managers Think," *Harvard Business Review*. November–December, 1984, pp. 81–90.

Jain, N., "Top Ten Lessons for an Entrepreneur," *Forbes*. June 16, 2011.

James, W., *The Varieties of Religious Experience*. New York: Mentor, 1958.

Jay, M., "The Secrets of Resilience." *Wall Street Journal*. November 11, 2017, pp. C1–C2.

Jobs, S., "'You've Got to Find What You Love,' Jobs Says," *Stanford News*. June 14, 2005.

Jordan, D. S., *The Philosophy of Hope*. San Francisco: Paul Elder and Company, 1907.

Jordan, D. S., *Standeth God within the Shadow*. New York: Thomas Y. Crowell and Company, 1901.

Jordan, D. S., *The Strength of Being Clean*. New York: H. M. Caldwell, 1900.

Keen, S., *What to Do When You're Bored and Blue*. New York: Wyden, 1980.

Kern, J. A., *Vision and Power*. New York: Fleming H. Revell Company, 1915.

Kheriaty, A., "Dying of Despair," *First Things*. August/September, 2017, pp. 21–25.

King, H. C., *Fundamental Questions*. New York: Macmillan Company, 1917.

King, H. C., *It's All in the Day's Work*. New York: Macmillan Company, 1916.

King, H. C., *The Laws of Friendship, Human and Divine*. New York: Macmillan Company, 1909.

King, H. C., *Letters on the Greatness and Simplicity of the Christian Faith*. Boston: Pilgrim Press, 1909.

Kluger, J., "Lent and the Science of Self-Denial," *Time*. February 23, 2012.

Koenig, H., "Religion, Spirituality, and Health: the Research and Clinical Implications," *International Scholarly Research Network*. Vol. 2012, ID 278730, 33 pages.

Koenig, H., "Research on Religion, Spirituality and Mental Health: a Review," *Canadian Journal of Psychiatry*. Pre-publication copy (2008).

Konner, M., "In Tough Times, Religion Can Offer a Sturdy Shelter," *Wall Street Journal*. July 1, 2017, p. C2.

Krause, N., and Ellison, C., "Forgiveness by God, Forgiveness by Others, and Psychological Well-being in Late Life," *Journal for the Scientific Study of Religion.* Vol. 40, number 1, 2003, pp. 77-93.

Kwilecki, S., "New Light on a Lost Cause: Atticus G. Haygood's Universalizing Spirituality," *Religions.* Vol. 3, 2012, pp. 357–368.

Luks, A., *The Healing Power of Doing Good.* Lincoln, NE: iUniverse, 2001.

Lucas, B., and Nordgren, L., "People Underestimate the Value of Persistence for Creative Performance," *Journal of Personality and Social Psychology.* Vol. 109, No. 2, 2015, pp. 232–243.

Mann, H., "Sixth Annual Report of the Secretary of the Board of Education," *The Common School Journal.* Vol. 5, number 18, September 15, 1843, pp. 280–288.

Mann, H., *Twelve Sermons.* Boston: Ticknor and Fields, 1861.

Marsden, G., *The Soul of the American University.* New York: Oxford University Press, 1994.

Maxcy, J., *American Eloquence.* New York: Alexander V. Blake, 1845.

Maxcy, J., *Collegiate Addresses.* London: Longman, Brown and Company, 1820.

McAfee, S., "Quoting Baseball: the Intellectual Take on Our National Pastime," *NINE: a Journal of Baseball History and Culture.* Vol. 13, number 2, Spring 2005, pp. 82–83.

McCleary, R. M., and Barro, R.J., *The Wealth of Religions: The Political Economy of Believing and Belonging.* Princeton, NJ: Princeton University Press, 2019.

McConnell, F. J., *Christian Focus*. New York: Eaton and Main, 1911.

McConnell, F. J., *The Preacher and the People*. New York: Abingdon Press, 1922.

McConnell, K., Gear, M., and Pargament, K., "Transgression and Transformation, Spiritual Resources for Coping with a Personal Offense," *Research in the Social Scientific Study of Religion*, Vol. 17. Boston, Brill Academic Publishers, 2007, pp. 49–77.

McCosh, J., *Certitude, Providence, and Prayer*. New York: Charles Scribner's Sons, 1883.

McCosh, J., *Gospel Sermons*. New York: Robert Carter and Brothers, 1888.

McDowell, W. F., *This Mind*. New York: Methodist Book Concern, 1922.

McMinn, M., *The Science of Virtue*. Grand Rapids, MI: Brazos Press, 2017.

McMinn, M., Snow, K., and Orton, J., "Counseling and Psychotherapy Within and Across Faith Traditions," in P. Nathan, ed., *The Oxford Handbook of Psychology and Spirituality*. New York and Oxford: Oxford University Press, 2012, pp. 255–270.

Miller, L., *The Spiritual Child*. New York: St. Martin's Press, 2015.

Montague, M.P., *Twenty Minutes of Reality*. New York: Dutton, 1917.

Moore, P., "Religious Conservatives Split on 'Benedict Option'," *YouGov.com*. December 3, 2015.

Mowrer, O. H., *The Crisis in Psychiatry and Religion*. New York: Van Nostrand Reinhold, 1961.

Muggeridge, M., *A Third Testament*. Boston: Little, Brown, 1976.

Nevin, J. W., *College Chapel Sermons*. Philadelphia: Reformed Church Publication House, 1891.

Newberg, A., *The Spiritual Brain: Science and Religious Experience*. Chantilly, VA: The Teaching Company, 2012.

Newport, F., "More U.S. Protestants Have No Specific Denominational Identity," *Gallup Religion*. July 18, 2017.

Nixon, R., *Six Crises*. New York: Pocket Books, 1962.

North. S., *Diligence in Business*. Utica, NY: Roberts, Printer, Oneida Herald Office, 1852.

Ohmann, O. A., "Retrospective Commentary," *Harvard Business Review*. January–February, 1970, p. 6.

Ohmann, O. A., "Skyhooks," *Harvard Business Review*. May–June, 1955, pp. 33–41.

Olin, S., *The Works of Stephen Olin*, Vols. I and II. New York: Harper and Brothers, 1852.

Peck, M.S., *The Road Less Traveled*. New York: Simon and Schuster, 1978.

Petersen, A., "Students Flood College Mental Health Centers." *Wall Street Journal*. October 10, 2016, p. D1.

Pinker, S., "When We Display Our Piety, Our Social Stock Rises," *Wall Street Journal*. October 20, 2016, p. C2.

Porter, N., *The Elements of Moral Science*. New York: Charles Scribner's Sons, 1893.

Porter, N., *Fifteen Years in the Chapel of Yale College*. New York: Charles Scribner's Sons, 1888.

Pritchett, H. S., *Andrew Carnegie: an Anniversary Delivered before the Massachusetts Institute of Technology*. Cleveland, privately printed, 1915.

Pritchett, H. S., *What Is Religion?* Boston: Houghton, Mifflin and Company, 1906.

Reed, J., "Turning Negativity into Creativity," *Success*. September, 2012, pp. 52–57.

Rehak, J., "Tylenol Made a Hero of Johnson & Johnson: The Recall That Started Them All," *International Herald Tribune*. March 23, 2002.

Richards, P. S., and Bergin, A. E., *A Spiritual Strategy for Counseling and Psychotherapy*. Washington, DC: American Psychological Association, 1998.

Robinson, E. G., *Principles and Practice of Morality*. Boston: Silver, Burdett, 1890.

Rosenzweig, S., "Some implicit Common Factors in Diverse Methods of Psychotherapy: At last the Dodo said, 'Everybody has won and all must have prizes.'" *American Journal of Orthopsychiatry*. Vol. 6, pp. 412–415.

Rotter, J., "Trust and Gullibility," *Psychology Today*. (October, 1980), p. 35+.

Satel, S., "Taking on the Scourge of Opioids," *National Affairs*. Summer, 2017, pp. 3–22.

Savino, M., and Mills, A., "The Rise and Fall of Moral Treatment in California Psychiatry, 1852–1870," *Journal of the History of Behavioral Sciences*. October 1967, pp. 359–369.

Schneider, H., and Schneider, C., eds., *Samuel Johnson, His Career and Writings*. New York: Columbia University Press, 1929.

Seelye, J. H., *The Source of Light and the Condition of Life*. Boston: Ginn and Company, 1889.

Seelye, J. H., *The Way, the Truth, and the Life*. Boston: Congregational Publishing Society, 1873.

Shannon, W., ed., *The Hidden Ground of Love: Letters of Thomas Merton*. New York: Farrar, Straus, Giroux, 1993.

Shulevitz, J., "The Lethality of Loneliness," *New Republic*. May 27, 2013, pp. 22–29.

Simpson, M., *Funeral Address Delivered at the Burial of President Lincoln*. New York: Carlton and Porter, 1865.

Small, A. W., "William Rainey Harper, The Man," *The Standard*, January 20, 1906, pp. 63–71.

Smith, A. D., *Letters to a Young Student*. Boston: Perkins and Marvin, 1832.

Smith, A. D., *Prayer as a Power*. Concord, NH: Republican Press Association, 1873.

Smith, A. D., *Success in Life*. Concord, NH: McFarland and Jenks, 1869.

Smith, S. S., *The Lectures, Corrected and Improved, which Have Been Delivered for a Series of Years in the College of New Jersey*, Vols. I and II. New York: Whiting and Watson, 1812.

Solzhenitsyn, A., "Repentance and Self-Limitation," in A. Solzhenitsyn, ed., *From Under the Rubble*. New York: Bantam, 1976.

Solzhenitsyn, A., "The Smatterers," in A. Solzhenitsyn, ed., *From Under the Rubble*. New York: Bantam, 1976.

Solzhenitsyn, A., *A World Split Apart*. New York: Harper & Row, 1978.

Sperry, L., "Spiritually Sensitive Psychotherapy: an Impending Paradigm Shift in Theory and Practice," in P. Nathan, ed., *The Oxford Handbook of Psychology and Spirituality*. New York and Oxford: Oxford University Press, 2012, pp. 223–233.

"Spiritual Treatment Eyed as Possible Treatment for PTSD," *Associated Press*. February 8, 2017.

Strauss, R., "Mind over Misery," *Stanford Magazine*. September/October, 2013, pp. 46–53.

Strawbridge, W. J., Selma, S. J., Cohen, R. D., and Kaplan, G.A., "Religious Attendance Increases Survival by Improving and Maintaining Good Health Behaviors, Mental Health, and Social Relationships," *Annals of Behavioral Medicine*. Vol. 23, number 1, pp. 68–74.

Strong, A. H., *One Hundred Chapel Talks to Theological Students*. Philadelphia: Griffith and Rowland Press, 1913.

Strong, A. H., *Philosophy and Religion*. New York: A. C. Armstrong and Son, 1888.

Stryker, M. W., *Baccalaureate Sermons*. Utica, NY: William T. Smith and Company, 1905.

Tappan, E., *Heroes of Progress*. Boston: Houghton Mifflin Company, 1921.

Taylor, C., *A Secular Age*. Cambridge, MA: Harvard University Press, 2007.

Taylor, E., *Shadow Culture*. Washington, DC: Counterpoint, 1999.

Thwing, C. F., *Letters from a Father to His Son Entering College*. New York: Platt and Peck, 1912.

Thwing, C. F., *A Liberal Education and a Liberal Faith*. New York: Baker and Taylor, 1903.

Tough, P., *How Children Succeed*. New York: Mariner Books, 2012.

Trumbull, J., and Dwight, S.E., "A Memoir of the Life of the Author," in T. Dwight, *Theology: Explained and Defended in a Series of Sermons*. Middletown, CT: Clark and Lyman, 1818.

Van Vranken, A., *Union College*, Vol. I. New York: Lewis Publishing Company, 1907.

Vitz, P., *Psychology as Religion*. Grand Rapids, Eerdmans, 1977.

Wagenseller, J., "Spiritual Aspects of Jungian Analytical Psychology: Individuation, Jung's Psychological Equivalent of a Spiritual Journey," in P. Nathan, ed., *The Oxford Handbook of Psychology and Spirituality*. New York and Oxford: Oxford University Press, 2012, pp. 286–303.

Walker, J., *Reason, Faith, and Duty*. Boston: Roberts Brothers, 1879.

Wallace, J., "An Attitude of Gratitude," *Wall Street Journal*. February 23, 2018, pp. C1–C2.

Washington, B. T., *Up from Slavery: an Autobiography*. New York: A. L. Burt, 1901.

Watson, J. B., *Behaviorism* (revised from 1924 edition). Chicago: University of Chicago Press, 1930.

Wayland, F., *The Elements of Moral Science*. Boston: Gould and Lincoln, 1852.

Wayland, F., and Wayland, H., *The Life and Labors of Francis Wayland*, Vol. 1. New York: Sheldon and Company, 1867.

West, J., and Stanovich, K., "Cognitive Sophistication Does Not Attenuate the Bias Blind Spot." *Journal of Personality and Social Psychology*. Vol. 103, number 3, 2012, pp. 506–519.

Williams, F., *The Nature Fix: Why Nature Makes Us Happier, Healthier, and More Creative*. New York: W. W. Norton & Company, 2017.

Winchester, C. T., "Memorial Address," *Bradford Paul Raymond*. Middletown, CT: Wesleyan University, 1916.

Winship, A. E., *Horace Mann, the Educator*. Boston: New England Publishing Company, 1896.

Wood, P., and Randall, D., "How Bad Is the Government's Science?" *Wall Street Journal*. April 17, 2018, p. A17.

Woolsey, T., *The Religion of the Present and of the Future*. New York: Charles Scribner and Company, 1871.

Woolsey, T., *The Religion of the Present and of the Future (rev)*. New York: Charles Scribner's Sons, 1887.

Worthington, E. L., *et al.*, "Forgiveness, Health, and Well-Being: A Review of Evidence for Emotional versus Decisional Forgiveness, Dispositional Forgivingness, and Reduced Forgiveness," *Journal of Behavioral Medicine*. Vol. 30, number 4, pp. 291–302.

Wrzesniewski, A., and Dutton, J., "Crafting a Job: Revisioning Employees as Active Crafters of their Work," *Academy of Management Review*. 2001, Vol. 26, number 2, pp. 179–201.

Zauzmer, J., "Why a Yale Neurologist Decided to Change Careers – and Is Now Becoming a Priest," *Washington Post* (blog). March 3, 2017.

ENDNOTES

1   *Evolution and Religion*, p. 59.
2   *Abba Father*, p. 8.
3   *Scholarship and Service*, pp. 195–196.
4   F. Carter, *Mark Hopkins*, p. 194. Hopkins was paraphrasing a sermon that had impressed him.
5   *Miscellaneous Essays and Discourses*, pp. 401–402.
6   *Honesty*, p. 8.
7   *Baccalaureate Sermons*, p. 66.
8   *The Elements of Mental and Moral Philosophy*, p. 267.
9   *Sermons and Addresses*, p. 134.
10 *This Mind*, pp. 22–23.
11 *Sermons and Speeches*, p. 136.
12 *Funeral Address Delivered at the Burial of President Lincoln.*
13 G. Marsden, *The Soul of the American University*, pp. 199–201.
14 An 1846 *Address to the People of Massachusetts on the Present Condition and Claims of the Temperance Reformation* by Williams College president Mark Hopkins typified the early college presidents' interest in treating alcoholism and lent credibility to self-help groups like the Washingtonian Movement for men.
15 M. Savino and A. Mills, A., "The Rise and Fall of Moral Treatment in California Psychiatry, 1852–1870."
16 *The Way, the Truth, and the Life*, Introductory Note.
17 Account of the convention taken from J. Barrows, ed., *The World's Parliament of Religions: An Illustrated and Popular Story of the World's First Parliament of Religions, Held in Chicago in Connection with the Columbia Exposition of 1893*, Vols. I and II.

18   The idea that a Christian might best express his or her faith through the world, rather than away from it was not entirely unique to America. Late eighth and ninth century medieval Christian writers had argued that for the possibility of a secular ministry, living spiritually in the material world by framing one's daily activities with readings on virtue. The Italian Renaissance similarly advanced the ideal of "civic humanism," serving God in the larger world by immersing oneself in classical art and literature—as if religious values could be absorbed by cultural osmosis. But Renaissance Italy was a homogeneous society. What the early college presidents saw in ecumenical movements was the opportunity for a broader field of action.

19   E. Taylor, *Shadow Culture*, p. 178.

20   R. Dubiel, *The Road to Fellowship*, p. 4.

21   E. Taylor, *Shadow Culture*, p. 179.

22   *Miscellaneous Essays and Discourses*, pp. 99–100.

23   *The College Year*, p. 201.

24   *Behaviorism*, p. 82.

25   J. Burtchaell, *The Dying of the Light*, pp. 144–145.

26   T. Woolsey, *The Religion of the Present and of the Future*, p. 289; and J. Walker, *Reason, Faith, and Duty*, pp. 151–152.

27   S. Rosenzweig, "Some Implicit Common Factors in Diverse Methods of Psychotherapy."

28   W. J. Strawbridge, S. J. Selma, R. D. Cohen, and G. A. Kaplan, "Religious Attendance Increases Survival by Improving and Maintaining Good Health Behaviors, Mental Health, and Social Relationships."

29   In A. Kheriaty, "Dying of Despair," p. 22.

30   Source: "Behavioral Health Trends in the United States," U.S. Department of Health and Human Services.

31   Source: U.S. Substance Abuse and Mental Health Services Administration (SAMHSA).

32   In A. Kheriaty, "Dying of Despair," p. 22.

33   In S. Satel, "Taking on the Scourge of Opioids," p. 3.

34   "Confidence in Institutions."

35   "2017 Edelman Trust Barometer Reveals Global Implosion of Trust."

36   *Sermon Occasioned by the Death of Miss Mary S. Dwight*, p. 15.

37   In P. Wood and D. Randall, "How Bad is the Government's Science?"

38   "On the Conflicts between Biological and Social Evolution and between Psychology and Moral Tradition," p. 1103.

39   In M. Konner, "In Tough Times, Religion Can Offer a Sturdy Shelter."

40   In H. Koenig, "Religion, Spirituality, and Health: the Research and Clinical Implications," p. 2.

41   In E. Taylor, *Shadow Culture*, p. 5.

42   In R. Strauss, "Mind over Misery," p. 49.

43   In R. Strauss, "Mind over Misery," p. 48.

44   In L. Sperry, "Spiritually Sensitive Psychotherapy: an Impending Paradigm Shift in Theory and Practice," p. 224 and 231.

45   "Orthodox Christians Must Now Learn to Live as Exiles in Our Own Country," *Time*.

46   In F. Newport, "More U.S. Protestants Have No Specific Denominational Identity."

47   Things Learned by Living, p. 200.

48   *A Liberal Faith and a Liberal Education*, pp. 156–157.

49   *Abba Father: or, The Religion of Everyday Life*, pp. 12–13.

50   *Prayers Offered in Wellesley College Chapel*, p. 25.

51   *Prayer as a Power*, pp. 23–25.

52   *The Spiritual Brain: Science and Religious Experience*, lectures 10 and 11.

53   *Abba Father: or, The Religion of Everyday Life*, p. 8.

54   *A Liberal Education and a Liberal Faith*, p. 146.

55   *A Liberal Education and a Liberal Faith*, pp. 144–145.

56   *Reason, Faith, and Duty*, pp. 98–99.

57   In M. McMinn, K. Snow, and J. Orton, "Counseling and Psychotherapy Within and Across Faith Traditions," p. 258.

58   *Fifteen Years in the Chapel of Yale College*, pp. 218–219.

59   *The Preacher and the People*, p. 73.

60   *Religion and the Higher Life: Talks to Students*, p. 153.

61   J. Dowd, *Life of Braxton Craven* (1896 edition), p. 198.

62   *Reason, Faith and Duty*, p. 257.

63   *College Chapel Sermons*, pp. 184–185.

64   J. Dowd, *Life of Braxton Craven* (1896 edition), p. 162.

65   J. Dowd, *Life of Braxton Craven* (1896 edition), p. 171.

66   Paraphrase of Matthew Simpson in G. Crooks, ed., *Sermons by Bishop Matthew Simpson*, p. 44.

67   G. Crooks, ed., *Sermons by Bishop Matthew Simpson*, p. 44.

68   *What Is Religion?* pp. 88–89.

69   *Sermons*, Vol. I, pp. 516–521.

70   *A Liberal Education and a Liberal Faith*, p. 121.

71   *Prayers Offered in the Wellesley College Chapel*, p. 25.

72   *Prayers Offered in the Wellesley College Chapel*, p. 25.

73   E. F. Dempsey, ed., *Wit and Wisdom of Warren Aiken Candler*, p. 169.

74   F. Fiske, ed., *Recollections of Mary Lyon*, pp. 221–222.

75   *Baccalaureate Addresses*, p. 89.

76   *Acres of Diamonds*, p. 43.

77   J. Kluger, "Lent and the Science of Self-Denial."

78   *Knowledge and Wisdom*, p. 10.

79   *Scholarship and Service*, pp. 342–343.

80   "Sixth Annual Report of the Secretary of the Board of Education," p. 288.

81   *Baccalaureate Addresses*, p. 39.

82   *Philosophy and Religion*, p. 564.

83   *Fifteen Years in the Yale College Chapel*, p. 378.

84   *The Religion of the Present and of the Future*, p. 315.

85   *Certitude, Providence and Prayer*, pp. 20–21.

86   E. F. Dempsey, ed., *Wit and Wisdom of Warren Akin Candler*, p. 93.

87   L. Halsey, *A Sketch of the Life and Educational Labors of Philip Lindsley*, p. 11 and p. 38.

88   L. Halsey, *A Sketch of the Life and Educational Labors of Philip Lindsley*, p. 27.

89   "Cognitive Sophistication Does Not Attenuate the Bias Blind Spot."

90   *Success in Life*, p. 19.

91   E. Tappan, *Heroes of Progress*, pp. 12–13.

92   Richard Nixon quoting President Eisenhower in *Six Crises*, p. 253.

93   A. Petersen, "Students Flood College Mental Health Centers."

94   *Fifteen Years in the Chapel of Yale College*, p. 182.

95   Paraphrased from W. D. Hyde, *Gospel of the Good Will*, pp. 155–156.

96 *Beyond the Dream*, pp. 169–170.

97 *The Source of Light and the Condition of Life*, pp. 7–8.

98 L. Halsey, ed., *Memoir of the Life and Character of Rev. Lewis W. Green*, pp. 122–123.

99 *Thoughts of and for the Inner Life*, pp. 83–84.

100 F. Fiske, ed., *Recollections of Mary Lyon*, pp. 230–231.

101 Source: U.S. Census Bureau.

102 *Sermons and Speeches*, p. 317.

103 Paraphrase of Rochester Theological Seminary president Augustus Hopkins Strong in *One Hundred Chapel Talks to Theological Students*, p. 152.

104 Paraphrase of Rochester Theological Seminary president Augustus Hopkins Strong in *One Hundred Chapel Talks to Theological Students*, pp. 152–153.

105 *Letters to a Young Student*, pp. 135–136.

106 J. Dowd, *Life of Braxton Craven* (1896 edition), p. 199.

107 J. Dowd, *Life of Braxton Craven* (1896 edition), p. 198.

108 *Up from Slavery*, p. 138.

109 E. Tappan, *Heroes of Progress*, pp. 149–153.

110 *Letters from a Father to His Son Entering College*, p.76.

111 C. Connley, "Suzy Welch: This Is the One Trait That Separates Successful People from Everyone Else."

112 J. Dowd, *Life of Braxton Craven* (1896 edition), p. 178.

113 *Thoughts of and for the Inner Life*, p. 296.

114 F. Fiske, ed., *Recollections of Mary Lyon*, p. 231.

115 *This Mind*, p. 112.

116 *This Mind*, pp. 112–113.

117 J. Zauzmer, "Why a Yale Neurologist Decided to Change Careers – and Is Now Becoming a Priest."

118 "There's Always a Solution."

119 S. Pinker, "When We Display Our Piety, Our Social Stock Rises."

120 *Things Learned by Living*, pp. 189–190.

121 *It's All in the Day's Work*, pp. 58–59.

122 Quoted in J. Wagenseller, "Spiritual Aspects of Jungian Analytical Psychology: Individuation, Jung's Psychological Equivalent of a Spiritual Journey."

123 *Certitude, Providence and Prayer*, pp. 20–21.

124 *Andrew Carnegie: an Anniversary Delivered before the Massachusetts Institute of Technology*, p. 8.

125 *One Hundred Chapel Talks to Theological Students*, pp. 93–94.

126 Letter to James Forest, February 21, 1966. Reproduced in W. Shannon, ed., *The Hidden Ground of Love: the Letters of Thomas Merton*.

127 *Fifteen Years in the Chapel of Yale College*, p. 177.

128 *Grief and Duty*, p. 9.

129 In J. Dowd, *The Life of Braxton Craven* (1939 edition), p. 190.

130 *The College Year*, p. 48.

131 The primary source for Haygood's biography is S. Kwilecki, "New Light on a Lost Cause: Atticus G. Haygood's Universalizing Spirituality."

132 *Sermons and Speeches*, p. 314.

133 In A. E. Winship, *Horace Mann, the Educator*, pp. 11–13.

134 "The Secrets of Resilience."

135 In W. G. Bennis and R. J. Thomas, "Crucibles of Leadership," p. 11.

136 In M. Jay, "The Secrets of Resilience."

137 As an example, see C. Hazard, *The College Year*, p. 127.

138 *The Strength of Being Clean*, pp. 9–10.

139 C. Duhigg, "Wealthy, Successful, and Miserable."

140 From the video "Entrepreneur Is Grateful for Failures and the People Who Kept Her Believing," produced by the Theology of Work Project.

141 K. McConnell, M. Gear, and K. Pargament, "Transgression and Transformation, Spiritual Resources for Coping with a Personal Offense," pp. 50–51.

142 *The Spiritual Child*, pp. 3–4.

143 *It's All in the Day's Work*, pp. 20–21.

144 J. Dowd, *Life of Braxton Craven* (1896 edition), p. 173.

145 "Listening to Your Heart: How Interoception Shapes Emotion Experience and Intuitive Decision Making."

146 In G. Crooks, ed., *Sermons by Bishop Matthew Simpson*, p. 168.

147 *Things Learned by Living*, p. 193.

148 S. Pinker, "When We Display Our Piety, Our Social Stock Rises."

149 *The Works of Stephen Olin*, Vol. I, pp. 276–277.

150 *The Works of Stephen Olin*, Vol. I, p. 45.

151 *Fifteen Years in the Chapel of Yale College*, p. 177.

152 *The Quest of the Best*, pp. 102–103.

153 S. McAfee, "Quoting Baseball: the Intellectual Take on Our National Pastime."

154 Analogy from M. Greene, *Thank God It's Monday*, p. 45.

155 *Gospel Sermons*, p. 169.

156 *Letters from a Father to His Son Entering College*, pp. 65–67.

157 J. Dowd, *Life of Braxton Craven* (1896 edition), p. 148.

158 *Vision and Power*, p. 304.

159 *Baccalaureate Addresses*, pp. 51–53.

160 *Baccalaureate Addresses*, p. 68.

161 J. Bonnefon, A. Feeney, and W. De Neys, "The Risk of Polite Misunderstandings."

162 *The Lectures, Corrected and Improved, which Have Been Delivered for a Series of Years in the College of New Jersey*, Vol. 1, p. 307.

163 *Standeth God within the Shadow*, pp. 12–14.

164 *Thoughts of and for the Inner Life*, pp. 175–176.

165 *Thoughts of and for the Inner Life*, p. 176.

166 Charles F. Thwing, *Letters from a Father to His Son Entering College*, pp. 50–51.

167 Adapted from R. Hanson, *Resilient*.

168 T. Herrera, "Let Go of Your Grudges. They're Doing You No Good."

169 A. Brooks, "Nice People Really Do Have More Fun."

170 J. Brody, "Positive Emotions May Extend Life."

171 E. L. Worthington, et al., "Forgiveness, Health, and Well-Being: A Review of Evidence for Emotional versus Decisional Forgiveness, Dispositional Forgivingness, and Reduced Forgiveness."

172 Quoted in T. Herrera, "Let Go of Your Grudges. They're Doing You No Good."

173 A. Solzhenitsyn, *From Under the Rubble*, p. 136.

174 *Farewell Address to the Students of Hamilton College*, p. 4.

175 *Three Great Temptations of Young Men*, p. 320.

176 J. Duffield, ed., *The Princeton Pulpit*, p. 105.

177 *Collegiate Addresses*, pp. 83–84.

178   *Sermons*, Vol. II, p. 74.

179   *Science of Mind*, p. 349.

180   Bascom quoting the Roman poet Juvenal, *Science of Mind*, p. 350.

181   Herbert and Carol Schneider, eds, *Samuel Johnson, His Career and Writings*, Vol. III, p. 468.

182   *Gospel Sermons*, p. 123.

183   *Standeth God within the Shadow*, p. 10.

184   Personal communication from sergeant's therapist.

185   Quoted in O. Hobart Mowrer, *The Crisis in Psychiatry and Religion*, p. 98.

186   Quoted in P. Vitz, *Psychology As Religion*, p. 93.

187   *Fruitfulness on the Front Line*, pp. 147–148.

188   *Sermons and Addresses*, p. 91.

189   *Are You Human?* p. 62.

190   In J. Faber and J. King, *How to Talk So Little Kids Will Listen*, p. 93.

191   *The Elements of Moral Science*, p. 559.

192   N. Krause and C. Ellison, "Forgiveness by God, Forgiveness by Others, and Psychological Well-being in Late Life."

193   K. McConnell, M. Gear, and K. Pargament, "Transgression and Transformation: Spiritual Resources for Coping with a Personal Offense."

194   "Spiritual Treatment Eyed as Possible Treatment for PTSD."

195   *The Laws of Friendship, Human and Divine*, p. 7.

196   *Christian Focus*, p. 75.

197   *Fifteen Years in the Chapel of Yale College*, pp. 299 and 302.

198   A. Small, "William Rainey Harper, The Man," p. 64.

199   *Religion and the Higher Life: Talks to Students*, pp. 92–94.

200   J. Trumbull and S. Dwight, "A Memoir of the Life of the Author," pp. lxix-lxxi.

201   C. T. Winchester, "Memorial Address," p. 18.

202   F. Fiske, ed., *Recollections of Mary Lyon*, p. 220.

203   *The Evidences of Christianity*, pp. 208–209.

204   *Letters on the Greatness and Simplicity of the Christian Faith*, pp. 133–135.

205   A. Brooks, "Nice People Really Do Have More Fun."

206   A. Brooks, "Nice People Really Do Have More Fun."

207 E. Bernstein, "The Surprising Boost You Get from Strangers."

208 Account taken from *The Autobiography of Benjamin Franklin*.

209 *The Road Less Traveled*, pp. 291–292.

210 *Existential Metapsychiatry*, p. 170.

211 *Dialogues in Metapsychiatry*, pp. 24–25.

212 *A Liberal Education and a Liberal Faith*, pp. 101–102.

213 *Religion and the Higher Life: Talks to Students*, pp. 34–35 and 61.

214 "Trust and Gullibility."

215 Personal communication on February 28, 1985.

216 J. Shulevitz, "The Lethality of Loneliness."

217 A. Luks, *The Healing Power of Doing Good*.

218 *Fundamental Questions*, p. 116.

219 *The Philosophy of Hope*, p. 36.

220 L. Halsey, ed., *Memoir of the Life and Character of Rev. Lewis W. Green*, p. 407.

221 *Baccalaureate Sermons*, p. 77.

222 *Fundamental Questions*, p. 112.

223 M. Muggeridge, *A Third Testament*, p. 39.

224 *Gospel Sermons*, pp. 30–31.

225 *The Religion of the Present and of the Future* (rev), p. 352.

226 *Religion and the Higher Life: Talks to Students*, p. 58.

227 In G. Crooks, ed., *Sermons by Bishop Matthew Simpson*, p. 61.

228 In G. Crooks, ed., *Sermons by Bishop Matthew Simpson*, p. 61.

229 *A World Split Apart*, p. 35.

230 *A World Split Apart*, p. 59.

231 J. Reed, "Turning Negativity into Creativity."

232 J. Reed, "Turning Negativity into Creativity."

233 B. Lucas and L. Nordgren, "People Underestimate the Value of Persistence for Creative Performance."

234 *Diligence in Business*, p. 6.

235 In F. Fiske, ed., *Recollections of Mary Lyon*, pp. 220–221.

236 *What Is Religion?* pp. 46-48.

237 In P. Tough, *How Children Succeed*, pp. 61–62.

238 K. Hymowitz, "Is There Anything Grit Can't Do?"

239 *Baccalaureate Sermons*, p. 77.

240 *Christian Focus*, chapter 2.

241   *Principles and Practice of Morality*, p. 226.

242   *Sermons and Addresses*, pp. 134–135.

243   J. Berzoff, "Narratives of Grief and Their Potential for Transformation," p. 121.

244   See P. Richards and A. Bergin, *A Spiritual Strategy for Counseling and Psychotherapy*, p. 219.

245   Likely derived from Philippians 2:13, "For it is God which worketh in you both to will and to do of his good pleasure."

246   Material on Benedict option adapted from L. Andrews, "The Religious, Ambitious Lose Faith in America."

247   R. Dreher, "Orthodox Christians Must Now Learn to Lives as Exiles in Our Own Country."

248   P. Moore, "Religious Conservatives Split on 'Benedict Option',"

249   *Fifteen Years in the Chapel of Yale College*, p. 117.

250   Adapted from H. Koenig, "Research on Religion, Spirituality and Mental Health: a Review," p.6.

251   *Baccalaureate Sermons*, p. 94.

252   J. Duffield, ed., *The Princeton Pulpit*, p. 111.

253   *Three Great Temptations of Young Men*, pp. 313–314.

254   *Collegiate Addresses*, p. 44.

255   G. Marsden, *The Soul of the American University*, p. 102.

256   F. Wayland and H. Wayland, *The Life and Labors of Francis Wayland*, p. 388.

257   F. Wayland and H. Wayland, *The Life and Labors of Francis Wayland*, p. 265.

258   F. Wayland and H. Wayland, *The Life and Labors of Francis Wayland*, p. 217.

259   *The Gospel of Good Will*, chapter 4.

260   "Crafting a Job: Revisioning Employees as Active Crafters of their Work," p. 190.

261   *The Wealth of Religions: The Political Economy of Believing and Belonging.*

262   *Sermons and Speeches*, p. 136.

263   "Retrospective Commentary," *Harvard Business Review*, p. 6.

264   "Skyhooks," *Harvard Business Review*, p. 41.

265   "Top Ten Lessons for an Entrepreneur."

266   "Retrospective Commentary," *Harvard Business Review*, p. 6.

267 Isenberg's research from his "How Senior Managers Think."

268 "You've Got to Find What You Love."

269 "When We Display Our Piety, Our Social Stock Rises."

270 J. Rehak, "Tylenol Made a Hero of Johnson & Johnson: The Recall That Started Them All."

271 A. Van Vranken, *Union College*, Vol. I, chapter 8.

272 "The Smatterers," p. 277.

273 *Three Great Temptations of Young* Men, p. 330.

274 Unpublished manuscript.

275 *The Meaning of Education, and Other Essays and Addresses*, p. 51.

276 *Science, Philosophy, and Religion*, p. 251.

277 *The College Year*, pp. 48–49.

278 *Twenty Minutes of Reality*, p. 8.

279 *Twenty Minutes of Reality*, p. 9.

280 *Twenty Minutes of Reality*, p. 32.

281 *Twenty Minutes of Reality*, p. 57.

282 *Twenty Minutes of Reality*, p. 61.

283 *Twenty Minutes of Reality*, p. 97.

284 *The Elements of Moral Science*, pp. 167–168.

285 In J. Wallace, "An Attitude of Gratitude."

286 Reported in M. McMinn, *The Science of Virtue*, pp. 75–76.

287 *A Secular Age.*

288 *Vision and Power*, p. 140.

289 *Letters on the Difficulties of Religion*, p. 189.

290 Information on nature research taken from F. *Williams, The Nature Fix: Why Nature Makes Us Happier, Healthier, and More Creative.*

291 *American Eloquence*, p. 345.

292 In F. Fiske, ed., *Recollections of Mary Lyon*, p. 222.

293 *Sermons and Speeches*, p. 279.

294 *Religion and the Higher Life*, p. 8.

295 *Religion and the Higher Life*, pp. 147–148.

296 See her *Educational Reminiscences and Suggestions*, chapters IV and V.

297 *Twelve Sermons*, p. 167.

298 Quoted in D. Entwistle, *Integrative Approaches to Psychology and Christianity*, p. 39.

299 *Jesus' Way*, chapter XI.

ACKNOWLEDGMENTS

This book represents more than twenty years' research into the teachings of America's early college presidents and how their Christian-inspired ideas for living spiritually in the material world motivated an entire nation to accomplish miracles, large and small. Thanks to Google, many of the presidents' writings are now available online, but such was not the case when I started. My heartfelt thanks to the Yale Divinity School, which granted me a Research Fellowship and, along with it, invaluable access to the university's rare manuscript collections.

As my goal is to make the presidents' self-help prescription accessible to modern audiences—and to show how the science of psychology, once the enemy of religion, has increasingly become its servant—I am also indebted to the many doctors, researchers, and therapists who have generously shared their insights with me. I will always be especially indebted to Dr. Marvin Karlins, who early in my career believed I had something to say and who helped me develop the skills to say it.

Finally, I would like to express my gratitude to both my agent, Bruce Barbour, and Fidelis Books associate publisher Gary Terashita, who have given me the priceless opportunity to share my discoveries with you, the reader.